Prisons

CRIME, JUSTICE, AND PUNISHMENT

Prisons

Ann G. Gaines

Austin Sarat, GENERAL EDITOR

CHELSEA HOUSE PUBLISHERS
Philadelphia

Chelsea House Publishers

Editor in Chief Stephen Reginald
Managing Editor James D. Gallagher
Production Manager Pamela Loos
Art Director Sara Davis
Picture Editor Judy L. Hasday
Senior Production Editor Lisa Chippendale

Staff for PRISONS

Senior Editor John Ziff
Associate Art Director/Designer Takeshi Takahashi
Picture Researcher Gillian Speeth
Cover Illustration Janet Hamlin

First Printing

1 3 5 7 9 8 6 4 2

The Chelsea House World Wide Web site address is
http://www.chelseahouse.com

Library of Congress Cataloging-in-Publication Data

Gaines, Ann.
Prisons / Ann Gaines; Austin Sarat, general editor.
   p.   cm. — (Crime, justice, and punishment)
Includes bibliographical references and index.
Summary: Discusses the history and philosophy of incarceration and examines conditions in American prisons and such related issues as prison reform, riots, prisoners' rights, and more.

ISBN 0-7910-4315-0 (hc)

1. Prisons—United States—Juvenile literature. 2. Imprisonment—United States—Juvenile literature. [1. Prisons.]
I. Sarat, Austin. II. Title. III. Series.
HV9471.G35 1998
365'.973—dc21
                                        98-22353
                                          CIP
                                          AC

Contents

CRIME, JUSTICE, AND PUNISHMENT

Fears and Fascinations:

An Introduction to
Crime, Justice, and Punishment

By Austin Sarat

We live with crime and images of crime all around us. Crime evokes in most of us a deep aversion, a feeling of profound vulnerability, but it also evokes an equally deep fascination. Today, in major American cities the fear of crime is a major fact of life, some would say a disproportionate response to the realities of crime. Yet the fear of crime is real, palpable in the quickened steps and furtive glances of people walking down darkened streets. At the same time, we eagerly follow crime stories on television and in movies. We watch with a "who done it" curiosity, eager to see the illicit deed done, the investigation undertaken, the miscreant brought to justice and given his just deserts. On the streets the presence of crime is a reminder of our own vulnerability and the precariousness of our taken-for-granted rights and freedoms. On television and in the movies the crime story gives us a chance to probe our own darker motives, to ask "Is there a criminal within?" as well as to feel the collective satisfaction of seeing justice done.

Fear and fascination, these two poles of our engagement with crime, are, of course, only part of the story. Crime is, after all, a major social and legal problem, not just an issue of our individual psychology. Politicians today use our fear of, and fascination with, crime for political advantage. How we respond to crime, as well as to the political uses of the crime issue, tells us a lot about who we are as a people as well as what we value and what we tolerate. Is our response compassionate or severe? Do we seek to understand or to punish, to enact an angry vengeance or to rehabilitate and welcome the criminal back into our midst? The CRIME, JUSTICE, AND PUNISHMENT series is designed to explore these themes, to ask why we are fearful and fascinated, to probe the meanings and motivations of crimes and criminals and of our responses to them, and, finally, to ask what we can learn about ourselves and the society in which we live by examining our responses to crime.

Crime is always a challenge to the prevailing normative order and a test of the values and commitments of law-abiding people. It is sometimes a Raskolnikov-like act of defiance, an assertion of the unwillingness of some to live according to the rules of conduct laid out by organized society. In this sense, crime marks the limits of the law and reminds us of law's all-too-regular failures. Yet sometimes there is more desperation than defiance in criminal acts; sometimes they signal a deep pathology or need in the criminal. To confront crime is thus also to come face-to-face with the reality of social difference, of class privilege and extreme deprivation, of race and racism, of children neglected, abandoned, or abused whose response is to enact on others what they have experienced themselves. And occasionally crime, or what is labeled a criminal act, represents a call for justice, an appeal to a higher moral order against the inadequacies of existing law.

Figuring out the meaning of crime and the motivations of criminals and whether crime arises from defiance, desperation, or the appeal for justice is never an easy task. The motivations and meanings of crime are as varied as are the persons who engage in criminal conduct. They are as mysterious as any of the mysteries of the human soul. Yet the desire to know the secrets of crime and the criminal is a strong one, for in that knowledge may lie one step on the road to protection, if not an assurance of one's own personal safety. Nonetheless, as strong as that desire may be, there is no available technology that can allow us to know the whys of crime with much confidence, let alone a scientific certainty. We can, however, capture something about crime by studying the defiance, desperation, and quest for justice that may be associated with it. Books in the Crime, Justice, and Punishment series will take up that challenge. They tell stories of crime and criminals, some famous, most not, some glamorous and exciting, most mundane and commonplace.

This series will, in addition, take a sober look at American criminal justice, at the procedures through which we investigate crimes and identify criminals, at the institutions in which innocence or guilt is determined. In these procedures and institutions we confront the thrill of the chase as well as the challenge of protecting the rights of those who defy our laws. It is through the efficiency and dedication of law enforcement that we might capture the criminal; it is in the rare instances of their corruption or brutality that we feel perhaps our deepest betrayal. Police, prosecutors, defense lawyers, judges, and jurors administer criminal justice and in their daily actions give substance to the guarantees of the Bill of Rights. What is an adversarial system of justice? How does it work? Why do we have it? Books in the Crime, Justice, and Punishment series will examine the thrill of the chase as we seek to capture the criminal. They will also reveal the drama and majesty of the criminal trial as well as the day-to-day reality of a criminal justice system in which trials are the exception and negotiated pleas of guilty are the rule.

When the trial is over or the plea has been entered, when we have separated the innocent from the guilty, the moment of punishment has arrived. The injunction to punish the guilty, to respond to pain inflicted by inflicting pain, is as old as civilization itself. "An eye for an eye and a tooth for a tooth" is a biblical reminder that punishment must measure pain for pain. But our response to the criminal must be better than and different from the crime itself. The biblical admonition, along with the constitutional prohibition of "cruel and unusual punishment," signals that we seek to punish justly and to be just not only in the determination of who can and should be punished, but in how we punish as well. But neither reminder tells us what to do with the wrongdoer. Do we rape the rapist, or burn the home of the arsonist? Surely justice and decency say no. But, if not, then how can and should we punish? In a world in which punishment is neither identical to the crime nor an automatic response to it, choices must be made and we must make them. Books in the CRIME, JUSTICE, AND PUNISHMENT series will examine those choices and the practices, and politics, of punishment. How do we punish and why do we punish as we do? What can we learn about the rationality and appropriateness of today's responses to crime by examining our past and its responses? What works? Is there, and can there be, a just measure of pain?

CRIME, JUSTICE, AND PUNISHMENT brings together books on some of the great themes of human social life. The books in this series capture our fear and fascination with crime and examine our responses to it. They remind us of the deadly seriousness of these subjects. They bring together themes in law, literature, and popular culture to challenge us to think again, to think anew, about subjects that go to the heart of who we are and how we can and will live together.

*   *   *   *   *

There is perhaps no greater indication of the current state of our thinking about crime, justice, and punishment than the fact that the United States today has considerably more than one million persons in jails and prisons. Our response to crime has moved from an effort to deal with its causes to coping with its consequences. Getting tough on crime means more people are going to jail for longer periods of time. Once there, criminals find that the overriding penal philosophy has dramatically changed. We incarcerate rather than rehabilitate those who violate our laws, and the conditions of that incarceration can be quite harsh. Some prisons are old, overcrowded, and violent. Others, the so-called "supermax" prisons, rely on the latest technological innovations to control the most dangerous prisoners, who are kept in solitary confinement and under constant surveillance 23 hours a day.

Are we a safer society as a result of these changes? And, more important, are we a more decent society? *Prisons* helps answer these questions by taking us inside the walls to see and understand what it is like to be a prisoner. This book also provides a vivid history of incarceration, giving its readers insight into the reasons we punish as we do.

Among the important issues this timely and penetrating book addresses are the special needs and difficulties experienced by women behind bars. Can one philosophy of punishment be applied to all kinds of prisoners? And what rights should prisoners have? What claims do those who violate our laws have on the rest of us? By addressing these questions *Prisons* reminds us that who we punish and how says much about our society, that one way of measuring the progress of our civilization is to ask how we treat the least civilized among us.

NOTHING LESS THAN SHOCKING?

Around 5:30 on the morning of August 26, 1976, Clifford Bailey and three fellow inmates at the District of Columbia jail squeezed through a window from which they had removed a bar, climbed down a knotted bedsheet, and escaped onto the streets of the nation's capital.

Before the year was over, authorities had recaptured all of the men. At the time of their escape, three of them had already been convicted and one was awaiting trial for a felony. Now, charged with escaping from federal custody, they faced the possibility of serving an additional five years behind bars, paying a fine of up to $5,000, or both.

When the three who had previously been convicted—Bailey, Ronald C. Cooley, and Ralph Walker—stood trial together on the escape charge, they offered a novel defense for their actions: necessity. Conditions in the jail were so bad and so dangerous, they argued, that not escaping would have amounted to risking their lives. The defendants testified that inmates and sometimes even guards set fire to bedding, trash, and other objects and that these fires were allowed to burn, filling cellblocks with smoke. Bailey, Cooley, and other witnesses testified that guards beat the men with blackjacks, slapjacks (a steel insert in a leather shell), and flashlights and threatened to kill them. Walker, an epileptic, claimed he had received inadequate treatment for his seizures. In essence, the defendants maintained, their actions had constituted an escape not from custody per se but from the dangerous and inhumane conditions in the jail.

Although the trial judge refused to allow the necessity defense, the Court of Appeals for the District of Columbia believed that the decision was an error. The appellate court ruled that the government should have to prove that, in escaping, the defendants intended to avoid confinement, defined as the "normal aspects" of punishment, and not such "nonconfinement conditions" as beatings and rapes.

Whether or not one thinks such distinctions are valid (the U.S. Supreme Court, in a 1980 decision, ruled that the intent of the escapees was irrelevant, though Justice Harry Blackmun vehemently dissented), it is hard to miss the irony in the case of *United States v. Bailey*. We remove lawbreakers from our midst largely to make society safe; that the lawbreakers might feel compelled to escape back into our midst for *their* safety is a curious development indeed.

But are conditions in American prisons and jails as bad as Bailey and his companions claimed? What is life behind bars really like?

There are no definitive answers to these questions, as conditions at the nation's correctional institutions vary widely. Some prisoners do their time in reasonably safe and humane environments. Many others, however, experience a nightmarish world of danger and violence, a world in which prisoners cannot count on being protected by those who supervise and guard them but must rely on their own resourcefulness to survive. In this world, stronger inmates prey upon weaker ones, and assaults and sexual abuse are commonplace.

A year after the Supreme Court delivered its ruling in *United States v. Bailey*, Jack Henry Abbott described the ever-present threat of violence in prison in his book *In the Belly of the Beast.* "*Everyone,*" Abbott declared, "is afraid."

> It is not an emotional, psychological fear. It is a practical matter. If you do not threaten someone—at the very least—someone will threaten you. When you walk across the yard or down the tier to your cell, you stand out like a sore thumb if you do not appear either callously unconcerned or cold and ready to kill.

A guard tower, fences, and multiple coils of razor and barbed wire stand between inmates and freedom at the maximum-security federal penitentiary at Marion, Illinois.

Sometimes interpersonal disputes or racial or ethnic tensions (often against the backdrop of prison gangs) boil over in deadly violence. In some institutions certain inmates even perform contract killings of inmates or, sometimes, of staff.

When prison violence is serious, the weapon of choice is generally the homemade knife, or "shank," which inmates fashion from whatever pieces of metal they can find. Given that prisons and jails are supposed to be secure facilities, the abundance of knives in correctional institutions is surprising. In many facilities it seems that almost every inmate has one.

For an inmate targeted by a fellow prisoner, the

end can come quickly and unexpectedly. Abbott described such a scene in *In the Belly of the Beast:*

> Here is how it is: You are both alone in his cell. You've slipped out a knife (eight to ten inch blade, double-edged). You're holding it beside your leg so he can't see it. . . . As you calmly talk and smile, you move your left foot to the side to step across his right-side body length. A light pivot toward him with your right shoulder and the world turns upside down: you have sunk the knife to its hilt into the middle of his chest.

When inmates share cells, work side by side, eat meals together, and share exercise periods, there is abundant opportunity for one inmate to attack another. And, as a practical matter, guards at many institutions

From Justice Blackmun's Dissent in *United States v. Bailey*

The atrocities and inhuman conditions of prison life in America are almost unbelievable; surely they are nothing less than shocking. The dissent in the Bailey case in the Court of Appeals acknowledged that "the circumstances of prison life are such that at least a colorable, if not credible, claim of duress or necessity can be raised with respect to virtually every escape." And the Government concedes: "In light of prison conditions that even now prevail in the United States, it would be the rare inmate indeed who could not convince himself that continued incarceration would be harmful to his health or safety." . . .

There can be little question that our prisons are badly overcrowded and understaffed and that this in large part is the cause of many of the shortcomings of our penal systems. This, however, does not excuse the failure to provide a place of confinement that meets minimal standards of safety and decency. . . .

The real question in this case is whether the prisoner should be punished for helping to extricate himself from a situation where society has abdicated completely its basic responsibility for providing an environment free of life-threatening conditions such as beatings, fires, lack of essential medical care, and sexual attacks. . . .

If respondents' allegations are true, society is grossly at fault for permitting these conditions to persist at the D.C. jail. The findings of researchers and government agencies, as well as the litigated cases, indicate that in a general sense these allegations are credible. The case for recognizing the duress or necessity defenses is even more compelling when it is society, rather than private actors, that creates the coercive conditions.

cannot or will not break up inmate-on-inmate knife fights in time to save a life. In his book *Warehousing Violence*, Mark S. Fleisher quotes a prison staff member's recollections of a deadly knife fight:

The exercise yard at Corcoran State Prison in California. Whenever prisoners congregate—at meals, during exercise periods, or during work—there is the potential for inmate-on-inmate violence.

> I was the first on the scene. I stood in [the victim's cell doorway] and watched. A [staffer] came up right after me. We stood there. What can you do? We yelled at [him]. "Drop the knife, put it down," but he just kept stabbing [him]. Blood was everywhere, splattered on the walls, and it was running over the floor. He kept stabbing him until his arm got too tired to stab anymore. Then he dropped the shank.

Three years after Clifford Bailey's escape and a year before the Supreme Court's *United States v. Bailey* decision, Wilbert Rideau, editor in chief of *The Angolite*, the award-winning magazine of the Louisiana State Penitentiary, wrote about violence and sexual abuse in prison in an article titled "The Sexual Jungle." Drawing on his own experience as a prisoner serving a life sentence, and citing various studies and the views of experts, Rideau concluded that the sexual victimization of male inmates by other inmates is "an integral feature of imprisonment throughout the United States"—that "rape and other sexual violence are as much a part of the [men's] pained existence as the walls holding them prisoner."

Although correctional institutions are filled with men in the sexual prime of their lives, experts say that prison rape has less to do with sexual satisfaction than with the establishment of the aggressor's "manhood" at the expense of the emasculated victim. "The act of rape in the ultramasculine world of prison," Rideau wrote in 1979, "constitutes the ultimate humiliation visited upon a male, the forcing of him to assume the role of a woman."

And after the initial rape—or, in prison terminology, "turning out"—the victim can look forward to a bleak future because he has been identified as someone who can't defend himself. That future might include repeated sexual assaults by other inmates or virtual slavery to one inmate, generally the initial rapist, in exchange for that inmate's protection. In prison, Rideau revealed, the man who first "turns out" a particular inmate holds claim to that inmate; he can take that man as his "old lady" and compel him to perform any services that a wife might perform in free society, including cleaning, errands, or sex; force him into prostitution; or sell him outright to another prisoner. An inmate who goes against the unspoken law of the prison risks repeated beatings or even death.

Whether the sexual abuse and slavery that Rideau described 20 years ago remain an integral feature of imprisonment *throughout* the United States is difficult to gauge. At the very least, however, advocates for prisoners say that although there is a reluctance to discuss the subject, a "culture of rape" permeates many of the nation's prisons. Stop Prisoner Rape (SPR), a national nonprofit organization, estimates from published surveys that 364,000 rapes occur each year in American correctional institutions. In the vast majority of cases, the victims are adult males in prisons (196,000) or jails (123,000). But an estimated 40,000 juvenile boys are raped in juvenile or adult facilities, and 5,000 women are raped in prison, according to SPR.

Occasionally, media coverage of a specific case provides the general public a glimpse of the problem. In October 1997, for example, the *New York Times* reported on the case of a prisoner whose story sounds frighteningly similar to Wilbert Rideau's earlier descriptions.

Michael Blucker, then 24, arrived at the Menard Correctional Center in Chester, Illinois, in 1993 to serve a sentence for theft. Within two weeks, he claims, three men, members of a prison gang, entered his cell while the other prisoners were going to a meal.

Prison Versus Jail

Although the words are often used interchangeably, prisons and jails are not the same. Prisons are state or federal correctional facilities that house convicts serving sentences of longer than one year. Jails, on the other hand, are locally administered correctional facilities that mostly hold people who are awaiting trial or who have been convicted and sentenced to a year's imprisonment or less. Six states have combined jail-prison systems. Nationwide, 2.9 percent of state convicts sentenced to prison terms were actually held in local jails in 1995, according to the U.S. Department of Justice's Bureau of Justice Statistics; this was due to prison overcrowding.

Among the other functions jails perform are:

- detaining juveniles pending transfer to juvenile facilities
- holding individuals who have been cited for contempt of court, who must be compelled to appear as witnesses at a trial, or who are in protective custody
- readmitting probation, parole, or bail-bond violators pending the disposition of their cases
- releasing convicted inmates to the community upon completion of their sentences
- operating, in some jurisdictions, community-based programs as alternatives to incarceration.

Of the estimated 1,725,842 persons incarcerated in the United States at midyear 1997, about one-third (567,079) were held in local jails. The rest were held in federal and state prisons.

One of the men got behind him and began choking him with a cord. When he began to struggle, Blucker says, another of the men showed him two homemade knives and told him to submit or he would die. In the days following the initial rape, Blucker was repeatedly assaulted. Eventually he was turned over to the leader of the gang, who sold his sexual services to other inmates for marijuana, money, or homemade alcohol.

After being paroled in 1996, Blucker—who contracted HIV, the virus that causes AIDS, during his term at Menard—sued prison officials and guards, claiming that they had failed to take action when he informed them that he had been raped and forced to become a sex slave. In court, when his attorney asked him why he hadn't accepted an offer by prison officials to be transferred to protective custody—a special wing where inmates targeted by other inmates are celled—Blucker replied, "Basically it's not protective custody. . . .

AIDS and Prison

Surviving a prison sentence no longer means simply avoiding situations that could lead to deadly violence. In recent years, the danger of a quick death through stabbing has been matched by the risk of a slow end through disease.

According to a Bureau of Justice Statistics report released in August 1997, a total of 24,226 American inmates—2.3 percent of all federal and state prisoners—were infected with HIV at year-end 1995. (HIV is the virus that causes AIDS, a deadly disease that destroys the body's immune system.) Because it is transmitted sexually, HIV is a particular concern in men's prisons where rape and consensual sexual contact are common. Rates of infection are highest in the Northeast; nearly 14 percent of New York's prisoners were known to be HIV positive in 1995. Because more women enter prison infected, rates were also higher among female state inmates (4.0 percent) than among their male counterparts (2.4 percent). In the federal prison system only 0.9 percent were infected. Although the total number of HIV-positive inmates increased 38 percent between 1991 and 1995, that growth roughly matched the increase in the overall prison population (36 percent).

One-half of one percent of all American prisoners had confirmed cases of AIDS in 1995, a rate six times higher than the rate in the general population. And in the five-year period from 1991 to 1995, one-third of all inmate deaths were attributable to AIDS.

If they want, they being gang members, to have something done to another individual in another part of the prison . . . all they have to do is send word to their other gang members, and it will be done. . . ."

Guards, too, have expressed similar concerns. One guard commented:

> The balance has tipped out of our favor. We've got very little to hold over a man, over the inmates, that commands just the respect of everyday dealings that we used to. They're no longer afraid of us. Let's face it, the fear is on our part now, not on theirs. The cons always used to do it out of fear. Now we're the ones that are afraid.

On occasion, statements like the above have led observers to question who really is in control of the prisons. But if prison authorities at certain institutions cannot even guarantee a convict's personal safety, there is another irony to prison life: for all the dangers that

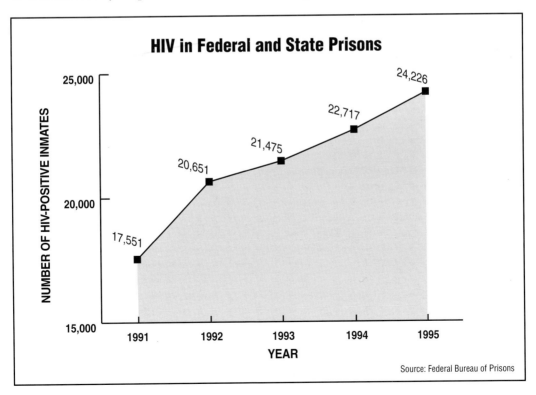

HIV in Federal and State Prisons

Source: Federal Bureau of Prisons

Playing handball against the 30-foot walls at Leavenworth Federal Penitentiary in Kansas. A world of danger, deprivation, and violence, the prison can also be a place of recreational amenities and special privileges, a situation many law-abiding citizens resent.

prisoners face, for all the humiliations they sometimes endure, they also enjoy rights and privileges that the rest of society does not automatically receive. For example, while millions of Americans have no medical insurance, prisoners are entitled to free, high-quality health care. While an estimated 26 million Americans sought food aid at shelters and soup kitchens in 1997 and as many as 5 million American children go to bed hungry each night, prisoners are entitled to three nourishing meals a day. They also have access to library facilities and at many institutions get free cable television and the use of a gymnasium and recreation rooms.

On the face of it, life for some prisoners seems easier than life for many law-abiding citizens. At Lompoc Federal Correctional Institute, a maximum-security prison in California, the day for most inmates begins with breakfast, served between 6:00 and 6:45 A.M. Monday through Friday. Breakfast consists of hot and cold cereal, toast, scrambled eggs, and fried bologna or Spam. After breakfast, prisoners return to their cells, watch morning TV, shoot pool, or socialize until 7:40, when everyone goes to work in a prison job or for an outside corporation that runs a factory within the prison perimeter. Wages range from $0.11 to $1.25 per hour, tax free. Work lasts until 11:00 A.M., when lunch is announced. Inmates must be back at work by 12:15 P.M. The workday is finished at 3:50, and everyone is back in his cell for a 4:00 count of the prisoners. The evening meal, which begins at 4:45, offers a wide range of hot foods: steaks, pork chops, fried chicken, and Mexican food are among the inmates' favorites. For both lunch and supper, a soup and salad bar is available. On weekends, the day begins at 7:00 A.M., when coffee and sweet rolls are served. At 10:15 brunch is served in a leisurely atmosphere and often includes eggs made to order, freshly cooked french toast or pancakes, sausage or bacon, fried potatoes, toast, and fruit juice; the salad bar is also available. After supper, inmates can visit their friends until 11:30 P.M. lights out. Weekend and evening activities include basketball or softball tournaments, action or adventure movies, and college-level courses; inmates also have access to both a law and a general library.

How did we arrive at this state of affairs, in which a prisoner may be subjected to extreme danger and deprivation or may be the beneficiary of a lifestyle that seems, to many citizens, more comfortable than a criminal deserves? What sort of treatment are lawbreakers entitled to, and how much money should be spent on them? More basically, what do we hope to achieve by putting criminals behind bars?

How we answer these questions defines, to a large extent, how we view ourselves as a society. To understand our current penological beliefs and practices, however, it is necessary to look into the past.

A Place
of Chains

Not until fairly recently did imprisonment emerge as the primary punishment for lawbreakers, but the use of prisons dates back nearly 4,000 years. One of the earliest known collections of laws was created in Babylon around the 18th century B.C. by King Hammurabi. The Code of Hammurabi regulated business transactions, property rights, and the rights of family members, including the relationship between master and slave. By today's standards, punishments were strict, even barbaric, and often involved mutilation or execution. If a son struck his father, for example, one of the son's hands was cut off. But the code also makes reference to prisons or dungeons for those convicted of debt, theft, or bribery. Ancient Egypt had prisons where inmates were forced to grind grain. In the Bible book of Judges, the Philistines force their Hebrew prisoner, Samson, to work grinding grain in their prison in Gaza.

Ancient Athens, the birthplace of democracy, had

Chained to a large wood block, a prisoner does time in an early English jail.

The biblical hero Samson is forced to grind grain in the Philistines' prison at Gaza. References to prisons date back almost 4,000 years, although the use of imprisonment as the primary punishment for crime is a relatively modern practice.

a prison called a *desmoterion*, "the place of chains," which was used to hold men until their fines were paid. Men who were condemned at trials, which by law could last no longer than a day, were executed in a number of ways, including being chained to the walls of the prison to die a slow death. In Plato's *Gorgias* dialogue, Socrates says about these condemned men: "[T]here they are, hanging up in the prison-house as examples to the world below, a spectacle and warning to all unrighteous men who come thither." This constitutes one of the earliest statements of the idea that prisons might serve as a deterrent—that the suffering of their fellow citizens might dissuade potential criminals from breaking the law, lest they too end up in prison.

In 451 B.C. the first written Roman laws, the Twelve Tables, gave the head of each household the right to maintain a family prison, the *ergastulum*, where slaves or disobedient family members could be held at the father's discretion. Outside of the family, however, the early Romans made little use of prisons except to hold debtors who were awaiting their sale into slavery. In cases tried before citizens or authorities, the penalty generally involved a fine or death. Roman law actually forbade the use of imprisonment as a form of punishment; prisons were to be used solely for the detention of suspects until their cases had been decided. Nevertheless, as the Roman Empire expanded across large areas of Europe and the Near East, provincial governors in particular relied on imprisonment to control the growing numbers of rebellious slaves and conquered peoples within the empire's borders.

After the fall of the Roman Empire in the fifth century A.D., the feudal system gradually emerged in western Europe. In England, after the Romans departed in the 440s and until the Norman Conquest more than 600 years later, the local Anglo-Saxon kings established and enforced the rules of society. Like their counterparts on the Continent, Anglo-Saxon kings owned vast estates that provided most of the revenue they used to run their kingdoms. In each county, or shire, the king appointed a "shire-reeve" (hence the word *sheriff*) to collect rents from his lands and, representing the king, to settle disputes and punish local criminals. The king usually chose someone he knew well or a member of the local landholding nobility to be the sheriff. Customarily, the appointment was for life and the position handed down from father to son.

Criminal matters were generally decided by what was called the "ordeal," by which a suspect was put through one of various barbaric tests that, it was believed, would provide physical "proof" of the suspect's guilt or innocence. In one form of the ordeal, for example, the suspect's head or hands were placed in boiling water. If the water scalded his or her skin, the suspect was judged guilty and executed; if it didn't, he or she was deemed innocent and released. In either case, justice was immediate, and there was no need for prison.

After the French Normans conquered Anglo-Saxon England in 1066, they imposed their own legal system on the country. Believing that the local nobility could not be relied upon to collect rents, the Normans replaced the old Anglo-Saxon sheriffs with men of lower rank loyal to the Normans; these men were trained in the traditional French legal service of the conquerors. Because the new sheriffs did not have the natural respect and position in the community that the previous nobles had, the power to judge and punish criminals was given to traveling courts, the *vicecomes*. These courts, which were also called eyres, would go from shire to shire. Often, months or years would pass before a suspected criminal could be judged.

It became necessary, therefore, to secure a person accused of a serious crime until the vicecome arrived in a shire. For this reason, King Henry II in 1166 required each sheriff to establish a "gaol," or jail, to hold those not yet condemned.

Early jails were often located in unused towers, cellars, or dungeons in the largest town of the shire. They usually comprised just one room without heat or sanitation. All prisoners—men and women, young and old—were kept together in the same crowded cell.

Prisoners were responsible for their own upkeep, including food and clothing, so they depended totally upon friends and relatives to keep them alive. A poor person or a person alone in the world could easily starve to death or die from cold while in jail. And all prisoners, regardless of their family connections, might succumb to one of the numerous diseases that plagued the jails. Many prisoners did, in fact, die in jail before their guilt or innocence had been established at trial.

At first, jail was used only to hold people until their case was heard—that is, until the traveling court arrived and conducted an ordeal or physical combat

between the accused and accuser. As with the Anglo-Saxon system, under early Norman justice those found innocent on the basis of "physical proofs" were immediately released, while those found guilty were immediately punished—typically by execution or corporal punishment. But after the Catholic Church banned the ordeal in 1215, authorities had to find another method for determining guilt or innocence. The method that emerged was the jury trial. In the early days of the English jury system, a person accused of a serious crime was not required to submit to a trial by jury but could instead choose to spend his or her life in jail. Many chose life in jail because a guilty verdict might result in an exceedingly painful execution. This caused the jails to begin filling up, which in turn led authorities eventually to compel all accused criminals to submit to a jury trial.

In the early days of English and European jails, dank, dark, and unsanitary conditions were the rule, and prisoners were responsible for their own food and clothing. Many inmates succumbed to cold, malnutrition, and disease before they got the chance to clear their names at trial.

Better to work
than stand thus

The establishment of bridewells in 16th-century England signaled a desire to find more humane ways of dealing with low-level criminals and the poor. In these county-run houses of correction, indigent women, prostitutes, and vagrants found shelter and work; the county received the profits from the inmates' labor.

Only seldom was imprisonment itself used as a form of punishment after a verdict. A statute from 1275 specified two years' imprisonment for rape. In 1285 a judge sentenced a lawyer who had lied in court to a year in the county jail. In 1361 a law was passed that called for two years' incarceration for stealing a hawk.

By the time of King Henry VIII, who ruled England from 1509 to 1547, a staggering number of lawbreakers, many of whom had committed only minor crimes, were receiving the death penalty. It is estimated that during Henry's reign 72,000 people were executed. This would be an average of 2,000 death sentences a year in a country with a population roughly equivalent to that of modern-day Arkansas. But despite all the executions, England's jails remained overcrowded, the primary

reason being that the country was undergoing fundamental social changes.

As the feudal system died out, many tenant families
of the old feudal lords were thrown off their small
farms. With no way to earn a living, these people soon
found their way to the growing cities, where many
could only beg. Vagrancy—having no place of resi-
dence or legitimate means of support—was itself a
crime, and other forms of petty crime increased enor-
mously. The old jail system, designed to handle a small
number of criminals charged with serious crimes, was
totally inadequate for a large number of petty criminals.

In 1553 King Edward VI gave a mansion called
Bridewell to the city of London to be used as a house
of correction for indigent women, prostitutes, and
vagabonds. In 1575 Parliament passed a law that
required a "bridewell" in every English county.

Although vagrants were generally still treated quite
harshly—punishments included whipping and boring
through the eardrum—the establishment of bridewells
signaled a desire to help the neediest of the desperate
poor: women and the very young, old vagrants who had
no means of support, people who had been forced into
petty crime by dire economic circumstances. In addition to fulfilling the function of incarcerating lawbreakers, they provided training, work, and some protection
from the extremes of deprivation outside. Bridewells
were the responsibility of the county, which provided
buildings and materials for the inmates' work. The
county, in turn, sold the workers' products. At Bridewell
in London, inmates spun cloth, baked bread, and made
tennis balls.

By the 1770s there were more than 200 jails,
bridewells, and other workhouses in England. It is
estimated that at that time 60 percent of the criminal
inmates were held for debt, 16 percent for petty offenses, and 24 percent for more serious felonies. There were
also some convicted felons serving sentences and some

insane people in jail. Many debtors' entire families lived in the jail with the father until the debt was paid. All prisoners mingled together in the cold and disease-infested semidarkness.

In 1773 John Howard (1726–1790) became sheriff of Bedfordshire. As a youth he had been captured by French pirates and held in a dungeon. Between beatings, he slept on a stone floor, and he subsisted on bread and water. The experience remained vivid to him throughout his life. After he was appointed sheriff, he visited the local jail and was horrified at living conditions in the cold and wet dungeon 11 feet below ground level. When he tried to correct the wretched state of affairs he found, local jail officials balked.

Howard left his home county and traveled throughout England, Scotland, and Ireland inspecting jails and searching for examples of more humane and productive treatment of inmates. He spoke before the House of Commons about the prison problems throughout the nation. In 1775 he went to the European mainland, where he hoped to find better jails. During his two-year trip covering more than 13,400 miles, he found that, in general, jail conditions on the Continent were actually worse than they were in England. However, in several places he found more enlightened treatment of criminals. At the Hospice of St. Michael in Rome there were small cells that each housed a single youthful offender. In Ghent, Holland, another jail had separate cells arranged in a pentagon around a control unit from which guards could supervise all of the prisoners.

Impressed with the new methods he found, Howard wrote a book, *The State of Prisons in England and Wales*, in 1777. In it he called for many reforms: separating men from women, the young from the old, the habitual criminal from the first offender.

In 1779 Parliament, swayed by Howard's appeal, passed the Penitentiary Act, intended to reform the British penal system. One of the act's provisions called

As their neighbors stroll by for a look, two colonial Americans sit in the stocks. Because maintaining prisoners in jail could be a financial burden, most colonial towns dealt with minor crimes such as drunkenness with punishments that involved public ridicule.

for a contest to design a new, more efficient jail. Although he didn't win the contest, another influential penal reformer, Jeremy Bentham (1748–1832), submitted a design intended not only to house prisoners in safety but to reform them. Bentham was a child prodigy who graduated from Oxford University at age 16. He was the founder of utilitarianism, a philosophy that tried to assess the value of all human acts according to their usefulness in everyday life. He felt that criminals would reform themselves if they had the opportunity to reflect upon their lives and actions. He designed a new prison called a "panopticon," from the Greek for "to be able to see all around." It was an eight-sided building with small cells filling each wall. Each cell was large enough for one person to sleep and work in. All cells could be watched from the central guard tower. Each prisoner would remain alone so that he could reflect on his past mistakes. Bentham called the panopticon "a mill for grinding rogues honest, and idle men industrious." In 1794 Parliament granted Bentham 2,000 pounds to start construction, but the panopticon was never built.

The British colonies in North America generally adopted England's penal system, just as they adopted other social institutions from the mother country. The first jail in the colonies was in the first permanent English settlement in America: Jamestown, Virginia. It was used to house several Indians in 1608 and a young German man in 1609.

At first, there was little need for jails in the colonies because there was little crime. But as the population grew, so grew the crime problem. The colonies responded in the tradition of their forefathers. Most towns constructed a jail that housed mainly those awaiting trial. These jails were under the direction of the local sheriff. Fines, whippings, and the restitution of double or triple the value of stolen goods were the usual penalties for minor transgressions.

Stocks, pillories, whipping posts, and dunking stools were often located next to the jail so that other minor punishments could be carried out immediately upon sentencing. The hope was that public ridicule would shame a wrongdoer into right conduct. Often, as a convicted criminal sat in the stocks or was dunked on the dunking stool, his neighbors pelted him with garbage.

The overriding factor influencing punishment in colonial jails was the cost to the community. Since each town had to pay for its law enforcement, the cheapest penalty was usually imposed. It was far cheaper to dunk a pickpocket than to hold him in a jail. And so the more immediate and, perhaps, the more humane punishment was the more common penalty for petty crimes. For more serious offenses, whippings were commonly administered to both men and women well into the 19th century.

REFORMING THESE UNHAPPY CREATURES

In 1787, the same year delegates from the American states gathered in Philadelphia to draft a federal constitution, the Philadelphia Society for Alleviating the Miseries of Public Prisons proclaimed its intention to construct a prison system that would "become the means of restoring our fellow creatures to virtue and happiness."

Throughout the late 18th and the 19th century, rehabilitation was the guiding principle for many American penal reformers, who saw in the frequently haphazard and inhumane conditions under which prisoners were housed a major impediment to transforming lawbreakers into productive citizens. More often than not, however, the prison reforms undertaken during this period spawned additional, unforeseen problems, bringing about another round of reforms.

The prominent Quakers who formed the Philadelphia Society for Alleviating the Miseries of Public Prisons were horrified at the terrible, chaotic condi-

A uniquely American institution, the penitentiary had its roots in Philadelphia's Walnut Street Prison (at left). Its founders, Quaker reformers, believed that "solitary confinement to hard labor"—as opposed to corporal punishment— along with "a total abstinence from spirituous liquors" would help reform wayward citizens.

37

tions of the local jails. Typically, prisoners of both sexes and all ages were locked up together in these crowded and unsanitary facilities, with the strong among them often brutally victimizing the weak. When necessary, guards maintained control through severe corporal punishments, such as flogging and even torture. Mere survival was a prisoner's major concern.

The Quakers recognized that this state of affairs was hardly conducive to rehabilitating a wayward citizen. Like Jeremy Bentham, they believed that quiet reflection on their mistakes would help prisoners to construct a better, more socially acceptable life. They persuaded the Pennsylvania legislature to designate Philadelphia's Walnut Street Jail a state prison for convicts from throughout Pennsylvania. In the new prison, the society declared, "solitary confinement to hard labor and a total abstinence from spirituous liquors will prove the means of reforming these unhappy creatures."

The Walnut Street Jail was a massive stone building constructed during the 1770s. It consisted of a two-story administration building that was flanked by two large wings. When it became a state prison, those convicted of misdemeanors or debt were held in one wing, and felons serving more severe sentences in the other. A new, three-story building was also constructed on the grounds of the old jail. Sixteen cells on its two upper floors held convicts sentenced to solitary confinement. A leading Quaker, Caleb Lownes, became the inspector of the prison and the manager of the various work programs set up in the prison yard.

The prison began operation in 1787. Inmates worked at shoe making, weaving, tailoring, sawing, and polishing marble, among other tasks. Men wearing brightly colored pantaloons were chained together and sent out into the streets of Philadelphia to work on public projects. In 1798 a school opened in the prison. In 1808 family visits were allowed to "prisoners who conduct themselves properly and are diligent in their

work." Religious instruction was also considered a vital part of the prisoners' schedule. A guard with a lit wick was stationed behind the preacher's pulpit at a cannon to ensure proper respect and attention during sermons. For those who would not follow the rules, the primary punishment was isolation. By 1818 those sentenced to solitary confinement could not leave their cells even to work and were not permitted to talk to the other prisoners.

This new prison represented a popular attitude in the United States, a nation flush with its sense of newly won freedom. It seemed that the proper duty of society was at least to try to seek out the basic goodness of the prisoner during his confinement. If it took the threat of a loaded cannon, that was all right too.

To a public that wanted reforms in an archaic penal system, Walnut Street Prison seemed an immedi-

When it opened, Cherry Hill Penitentiary in Philadelphia was the largest building in the United States, containing more than 400 cells, each with a walled outside garden. During their entire sentence at Cherry Hill, prisoners lived and worked in their own cells, remaining silent and never seeing another inmate. This, it was believed, would help inmates think about their past mistakes and reform.

ate success. By 1818 New York, Kentucky, New Jersey, Virginia, Massachusetts, Maryland, Vermont, New Hampshire, Ohio, and Georgia had constructed state prisons that were modeled on the Walnut Street Prison. By then, however, Walnut Street Prison itself was overcrowded and underfinanced. The Pennsylvania legislature authorized construction of two new, larger "penitentiaries" (meaning places that contained those who are penitent, or sorry), to be constructed on opposite sides of the state, one near Philadelphia, the other near Pittsburgh.

The new Philadelphia penitentiary, built on a cherry orchard, came to be called Cherry Hill (and, later, Eastern State) Penitentiary. It contained more than 400 cells, each with a walled outside garden. At the time it was the largest building in the country. The Pittsburgh prison soon opened with another 170 solitary cells. A warden described prisoner treatment:

> When a convict first arrives he is placed in a cell and left alone without work and without any book. His mind can only operate on itself; generally but a few hours elapse before he petitions for something to do and for a Bible. If the prisoner has a trade that can be pursued in his cell, he is put to work as a favour; as a reward for good behavior . . . a Bible is allowed him. If he has no trade, or one that cannot be pursued in his cell, he is allowed to choose one that can and he is instructed by one of the overseers.

Prisoners remained alone and silent for their entire sentence. They never saw another prisoner. To ensure total isolation, convicts entered and were moved around inside the prison blindfolded. When he visited the penitentiary, Charles Dickens, the famous English author and social critic, was horrified at the unspoken agony he observed.

> In its intention I am well convinced that it is kind, humane and meant for reformation; but I am persuaded that those who devised this system of prison discipline, and those benevolent gentlemen who carry it into execu-

Bang.

tion, do not know what they are doing. I believe that very few men are capable of estimating the immense amount of torture and agony which this dreadful punishment, prolonged for years, inflicts upon sufferers. . . .

Like the Walnut Street Prison, the Cherry Hill Penitentiary won immediate public acceptance but soon became filled to overcrowding. In Auburn, New York, in 1823, a new prison opened that was designed not to become overcrowded as quickly. The cells were designed to be significantly smaller than those at Cherry Hill so that more cells could be constructed at a reasonable cost. The smaller cells at Auburn were judged to be adequate because they would hold the prisoners only at night; prisoners would not be allowed to work alone in their cells. During the day, they would work together in several large shops. As in the Cherry

Convicts trade their civilian garb for prison stripes at New York's Sing Sing prison. An Auburn-style penitentiary constructed in the 1820s, Sing Sing was designed to be more economical than the Penn-sylvania-style prisons. It contained many small cells where prisoners slept; during the day they worked together in large shops.

Hill Penitentiary, silence was always enforced in Auburn, even at work and meals. To go to meals, to work, and back to their cells at night, the inmates marched in unison in a slow shuffle called the "locked step," one man's hand resting on the shoulder of the man in front. Everyone's head was turned over his right shoulder so that the guards could make sure no one was talking.

The cells, which measured 7 by 3.5 by 7 feet, had no windows. Iron bars were placed in the front of each cell, which kept the prisoners in constant view of guards. Those who violated rules even in the slightest way received severe whippings. More uncooperative prisoners were then placed in total solitary confinement. An English prison chaplain who visited Auburn described its effect on convicts:

> [A] few months in the solitary cell renders a prisoner strangely impressible. The chaplain can then make the brawny navvy cry like a child; he can work on his feelings in almost any way he pleases; he can, so to speak, photograph his thoughts, wishes and opinions on his patient's mind, and fill his mouth with his own phrases and language.

In 1825 the state of New York began construction, with 100 carefully selected convicts, of a second Auburn-style prison at Ossining-on-the-Hudson, a prison that soon became famous as "Sing Sing."

Louis Dwight, the founder of the Boston Prison Discipline Society, had visited many of the older New England jails, and he became a champion of the new penitentiaries. In 1827 his society supported the construction of an Auburn-style prison in Wethersfield, Connecticut, for a very reasonable $30,000. Within 10 years, other Auburn-style prisons were constructed in Massachusetts, New Hampshire, Vermont, Maryland, Kentucky, Ohio, Tennessee, and Washington, D.C.

Although the Pennsylvania, or "separate," system, and the Auburn, or "congregate," system of penitentiaries now appear very similar in their philosophy of rehabilitating the criminal and in their use of silence, a great public debate arose over which system worked best. In the Pennsylvania system, there were few disciplinary problems, since the convicts never left their cells. Fewer guards were needed, and guards had less impact on a prisoner's life. European visitors to the new Pennsylvania prisons were impressed by their seeming success. They returned to their homes and began reform movements that resulted in Pennsylvania-style prisons in England (1835), Belgium (1838), Sweden (1840), Norway (1851), and Holland (1851).

The Auburn-style prison, on the other hand, was cheaper to construct and often produced a profit through the convict labor pool. It became the more popular prison type in the United States. At $750,000, the Cherry Hill Penitentiary cost 25 times more to build than the Wethersfield Prison. Most state prisons in use in the United States today were constructed on the principles of the Auburn system, with massive stone buildings and walls with guard towers, huge cellblocks with many tiny cells, and large factories and farms worked by the convicts. This basic type of prison construction continued in the United States well into the 1960s.

The new penitentiaries were designed with the noble purpose of reforming inmates' lives. In practice, however, that was rarely the primary consideration. Guards and prison officials shared in substantial profits from convict labor, extortion, and the petty graft of selling favors and supplies. This led to many cruelties and abuses. Floggings and tortures, which the new penitentiaries had been designed to replace, returned to enforce strict rules and prompt greater production by the inmate laborers.

While men have always made up a vast majority of America's prisoners, the treatment of women inmates was a concern early on. A visitor to New York City's

Bellevue Prison in 1838 saw women walking the same treadmill as men to grind grain for the prison bakery. There were no provisions for separate treatment for female prisoners. At night, all prisoners slept in a common large cell. "Women," one observer stated, "stood the ordeal better than the men."

Nevertheless, in keeping with the prevailing view of women as the weaker sex, some 19th-century reforms that would eventually affect the way all prisoners were treated originated as efforts to treat women less harshly. The first step was to remove women from the general prison population. When the Cherry Hill Penitentiary opened in Philadelphia in 1825, both men and women were confined at the prison. Since each prisoner lived in isolation, there was no need to provide sep-

About three-quarters of America's women prisoners are mothers, and as many as 1 in 16 female convicts enter prison pregnant.

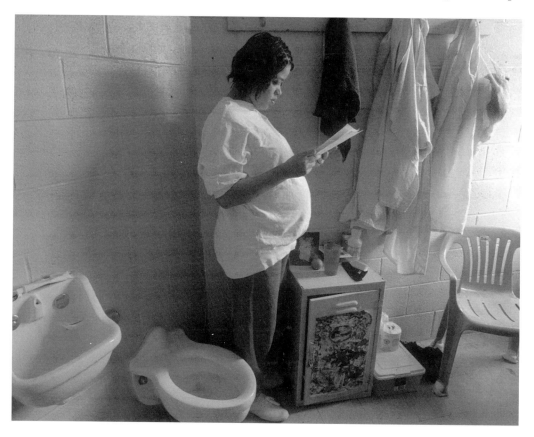

arate facilities. Soon, however, women at Cherry Hill received some considerations not given to men. They were supervised by a woman administrator called a matron. They were sometimes allowed visits from Quaker ladies who read to them from the Bible or gave them lessons in reading and writing.

In 1839 the Mount Pleasant Female Prison was opened on the grounds of the Auburn-style penitentiary for men at Ossining, New York. This was the first women's prison in the United States. In 1844, under the direction of chief matron Eliza Farnham, the prison began earning a reputation for its humane treatment. The women inside were encouraged to educate themselves. Classes were conducted in geography, literature, astronomy, and physiology. Farnham modified the rule

Women in Prison

Women have always accounted for a small percentage of America's prisoners—at midyear 1997 the figure stood at 6.4 percent. Though that percentage is up from 4.1 percent in 1980 and 5.7 percent in 1990, the rate of incarceration for men is still 16 times higher than that for women. In 1997 there were 78,067 female inmates in the more than 110 state and federal women's prisons and "coed facilities" (women's penitentiaries that are a part of a men's prison complex).

Women inmates are less likely than their male counterparts to have been convicted of violent crimes, and the typical profile of a female inmate is of a woman with little education and dim economic prospects. According to the California-based Prison Activist Resource Center, nationwide the average age of female inmates is 29, nearly 60 percent have not completed high school, and 8 in 10 report incomes of less than $2,000 the year before their arrest. The percentage of female prisoners who have been physically or sexually abused before incarceration may be higher than 40 percent, and one in three women in prison for homicide has killed a husband or boyfriend, often after a history of such abuse.

Women in prison endure special deprivations. About three-quarters are mothers, and an estimated 60,000 American children under age 18 have mothers serving prison time. In more than half of the cases, a female inmate will never see her children during her prison sentence. In addition, about 1 in 16 women enter prison pregnant. Even during childbirth, they are often handcuffed or shackled to hospital beds to prevent escape and are separated from their children soon after birth. Only a handful of women's prisons in the country allow an infant to remain with its mother after birth, and few prisons allow overnight or weekend visits by children.

As inmate populations soared after the Civil War, prison administrators relied on a variety of brutal punishments to maintain order. Shown here is a Georgia prison's "box," where the uncooperative were cooped up.

of silence and introduced flowers, music, and visits from family members to the bleak prison environment. Severely criticized for her policies, Farnham resigned in 1847. The prison soon became overcrowded and was closed shortly after the Civil War.

As early as 1852, the New York Prison Commission reported the failure of penitentiaries to rehabilitate prisoners. "[P]rotracted incarceration," it said, "destroys the better faculties of the soul."

One effort to change that began in Michigan in 1861, when a prison administrator from New York, Zebulon R. Brockway, was hired to direct Detroit's new men's and women's "House of Corrections." Brockway initiated several successful reform programs. He found jobs in the city for convicts who maintained good conduct during their sentences. In 1865 he granted wages to the convict laborers who reached production goals. In 1869 he opened a House of Shelter adjacent to the House of Corrections where women prisoners who had completed their sentences could stay and work until they found other employment. (Today it would be called a "halfway house.") Brockway soon moved some women prisoners to the House of Shelter so that they might complete their sentences in a more liberal and homelike atmosphere than that found in the House of Corrections.

In general, however, conditions in the nation's prisons remained dismal. By the end of the Civil War in 1865, there was little money for new prison construction but a growing number of convicts. As penitentiaries began housing three or four convicts in cells designed for one, thoughts of real reform disappeared, and prison administrators employed bizarre and brutal punishments to maintain order in institutions that were bulging at the seams. A nationwide survey of prisons in 1867 by Enoch Wines and Theodore Dwight revealed that order in America's prisons was being maintained with water tortures, whippings, cages, and extended periods of solitary confinement.

In the post–Civil War period, states (particularly in the South) began to pay for their prisons—and often make a considerable profit besides—by leasing prisoners' labor to independent contractors, who either operated factories inside the prison walls or took prisoners away to work on projects such as roads, railroads, canals, and mines. Some jails and prisons were actually owned and operated privately. How much work prisoners had to do—as well as how they were treated—was left entirely to the discretion of the contractor. Many prisoners were literally worked to death.

In an era of tight prison budgets, virtually all new prison construction the states undertook was designed to house as many convicts as possible in the least amount of space and at the lowest cost. These massive prisons became known as "Big Houses," and their cost-effectiveness is indisputable: in 1967 a total of 44 American penitentiaries built before 1900 were still in operation. Each Big House—San Quentin in California, Stateville in Illinois, Jackson in Michigan, to name some of the more famous—contained about 2,500 inmates. By 1929 there were 2 prisons housing more than 4,000 inmates each, 10 more had inmate populations greater than 2,000, and 18 others had more than 1,000 inmates each.

But isolated reform efforts continued. In 1873 the Indiana Reformatory Institution for Women and Girls opened in Indianapolis. It was the first women's penal institution administered entirely by women, and it reflected a double standard in the treatment of the sexes. With men, criminality, not immorality or unsavory habits, was what landed someone behind bars. But young women ages 16 and older who had been judged to "habitually associate with dissolute persons" were committed to the Indiana Reformatory, as were other uneducated and poor women. The goal of the new institution was rehabilitation, not punishment. It was stated that obedience to the rules and systematic religious education would help women there form orderly habits and embrace moral virtue. Massachusetts opened a similar institution, its Women's Reformatory, in 1877. The New York Reformatory for Women opened in 1901. The District of Columbia and New Jersey soon followed suit with women's reformatories of their own.

Prisoners at San Quentin line up in the main yard to go to dinner, 1934.

Another post–Civil War reform movement began among administrators of youth reformatories, who felt that they simply did not have enough time to rehabilitate their youthful charges. They lobbied various courts and state legislatures to adopt a new policy in sentencing young criminals: sentencing them to a state institution for as long as it took to rehabilitate them, not for a predetermined amount of time. This new type of open-ended sentence became known as an "indeterminate sentence."

In 1876 the Elmira State Reformatory for young men ages 16 to 30 opened in Elmira, New York, under the direction of the noted penal administrator Zebulon R. Brockway. Brockway had left his position as director of the Detroit House of Corrections in 1871 because he could not get an indeterminate-sentence bill through Michigan's state legislature. In New York, Brockway had the advantage of a more reform-minded legislature, which had recently passed a comprehensive indeterminate-sentence bill.

In many ways the Elmira Reformatory soon became the model for both reform schools and penitentiaries; by 1913, 18 other states had adopted the Elmira system. Elmira had a school, a library, a gymnasium, an athletic field, a glee club, and a newspaper published by inmates. Inmates received education in academic and job skills and were given moral instruction from the Scriptures. When they were not working, they wore military-like uniforms, carried toy rifles and swords, and marched in close-order drill to the tune of the inmate fife and bugle corps.

But the most significant feature about Elmira was the use of indeterminate sentencing. No one sent to Elmira knew when he would be released; its board of

Locking up Children

In the colonial era and during the first years of the Republic, it was widely believed that children seven years or older were morally developed and hence fully responsible for their actions. If they broke the law, they were punished like adults. Children who were sentenced to prison terms generally remained in local jails but were sometimes sent to penitentiaries. In both settings adult criminals frequently brutalized them.

Gradually, however, the belief emerged that children are not fully developed morally but are susceptible to the influences of their surroundings. As early as the 1820s reform-minded groups such as New York's Society for the Prevention of Pauperism began to advocate removing children from jails and penitentiaries, where they were exposed to the corrupting influence of criminal adults. In 1824 the society set up a "youth reformatory" in a remodeled military barracks. Two years later the state of New York took control of this facility. Soon other reformatories sprang up around the country, and by 1857 there were 17 of these "houses of refuge" containing more than 20,000 juveniles.

Despite being separated from the adult prison population, young offenders often suffered the same harsh treatment as their older counterparts. Loss of privileges was the common punishment for minor offenses, but some children were handcuffed and made to drag around a ball and chain. Whippings, managers decided when to free each prisoner based on his behavior at the reformatory. Each inmate received credits for work performed and good conduct. When an inmate had accumulated enough credits, he became eligible for parole.

In theory indeterminate sentencing—which soon became the norm for adult convicts as well as for youths—was a monumental improvement over previous penal policy because it made the prisoner responsible for earning his release. He no longer just waited; if he wanted to get out, he had to act in an appropriate manner. This not only made prisons easier to manage but also, presumably, taught inmates lessons about socially acceptable behavior—lessons that they might apply after being released.

Unfortunately, the policy of indeterminate sentencing was only as good as the prison officials who administered it. In the hands of administrators less enlightened than Zebulon Brockway, it became a

solitary confinement, blindfolding, and slow starvation might follow more serious offenses.

In 1899 the state of Illinois passed the Juvenile Court Act, which established the nation's first juvenile court and gave rise to new procedures for dealing with child lawbreakers. The stated goal of the juvenile system was always to do what was best for the child; treatment, not punishment, was the guiding principle. The idea was an immediate success. By 1917 all but three states had adopted juvenile courts; by 1945 all of the states had juvenile court systems.

When a child was adjudicated delinquent in a juvenile court (in keeping with the special mandate of the juvenile system, the term *guilty* was avoided), the judge decided how the child's treatment needs could best be met. A typical disposition might be commitment to a reform school, training school, or ranch until age 18.

Today, with the widespread perception that juvenile crime is out of control, punishment has become as important a consideration as treatment in dealing with young offenders. In 1991 more than 100,000 juveniles were incarcerated in prisons, jails, or juvenile detention facilities. An increasing number of juveniles are tried in adult courts and given lengthy sentences that they serve in part or in full in adult prisons.

fearful and arbitrary weapon. Prisoners could be—and sometimes were—locked up indefinitely based on the whim of guards or wardens rather than on any objective criteria. In many cases prisoners had no idea how long they would be incarcerated.

Although it was the general desire of penologists to rehabilitate all prisoners, women and children received the greatest attention. But in their zeal penologists often enforced measures that actually produced harsher and crueler punishments than the men received. Many state laws called for all women over 16 convicted of any offense to be sent to state women's reformatories. Although these laws were enacted to ensure that women were not sent to men's penitentiaries, they prevented judges from issuing short, local county jail sentences to women who had committed minor offenses. Instead, judges were forced to give all women indeterminate sentences at a state reformatory for women.

Minnesota law, for example, specified that women be sent to the reformatory "without limit as to time." A woman could theoretically serve a life sentence for the same crime that would land a man six months in the county jail. In order to redress the obvious injustice of this type of "forever" sentence, most state sentencing laws mandated a maximum sentence for each crime. In sentencing, the judge set an upper limit on the length of time an individual would serve. The prison administration would then decide exactly when to release a convict. In Pennsylvania, however, the Muncy Act, passed in 1913, made it compulsory for a judge to give women the maximum sentence provided by law for any crime so that the state's policy of rehabilitation would always have the maximum amount of time to do its work. In practice, women served more time under their indeterminate sentences than did men convicted of the same crimes.

In July 1968 the State Supreme Court of Pennsylvania ruled that the Muncy Act was unconstitutional.

Two weeks later the Pennsylvania legislature passed another law, worded slightly differently from the Muncy Act, that again established mandatory indeterminate sentencing for women. By the 1990s indeterminate sentencing had ended for adult women, but several states retained it for the young. For example, in New Jersey any person under 26 years old, male or female, could be sentenced to an indeterminate term of incarceration.

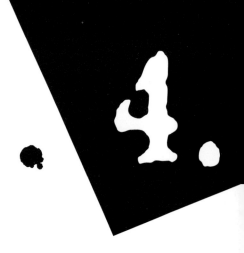

FEDERAL REFORMS

During the first century of U.S. penal history, virtually all the developments in correctional practices occurred within the states' prison systems. Indeed, it would be more than 100 years after the establishment of the United States before the federal government got its own prisons. But after entering the area of corrections, the federal system would lead the way in reform.

In 1776 the Continental Congress, as the first body to exercise the power of what would become the United States of America, authorized the arrest and imprisonment of Benjamin Franklin's son William for the charge of treason. As governor of New Jersey, William Franklin had offered to turn the colony over to the British army. When he was placed in the Litchfield, Connecticut, town jail, Franklin became one of the

Between 1934 and 1963, Alcatraz, which sits on an island in the middle of San Francisco Bay, housed the federal government's most "vicious and irredeemable" prisoners.

first "federal" prisoners.

In 1789 the newly empowered Congress established a federal court system to prosecute those charged with violating the laws it enacted under the powers defined in the U.S. Constitution. Without its own prisons, however, the federal government had to send its prisoners to state penal facilities and pick up the tab for their incarceration.

In the early years of the United States, there really was no need for a prison for federal convicts. An 1846 review showed only 48 federal prisoners, in large measure because there were few federal crimes. Murder, rape, and theft, for example, all violated state laws. Of the 48 federal convicts, 27 were sentenced for either mail theft or counterfeiting. Other federal crimes being punished at the time were mutiny at sea, slave trade violations, and attempting to incite a revolt. Federal marshals were instructed to find the most economical jails they could for their charges. In 1846 the cost of keeping each federal prisoner was between 16 $^1/_2$ and 28 cents a day.

Eventually the practice of leasing out convict labor—and the abuses this so-called contract system engendered—undermined the federal government's arrangements with the states. In 1875 the attorney general, Edwards Pierrepont, reported that "great wrongs are done and cruelties are practiced" on federal prisoners in state prisons. He went on:

> In some of the States the system prevails of letting the prisoners to work for cruel task-masters, and while the United States pay for the keeping of their prisoners from 70 cents to $1 each per day, these same prisoners earn a large amount of money, which goes to the keeper of the prison, and of which no account is ever rendered to the United States, while the prisoners are often driven a long distance to work for those who hire them, are improperly fed and clothed, over-worked, sometimes severely beaten for slight offenses, and are made a source of large profit to those who avail themselves of this kind of forced labor.

There were soon outcries by humanitarian groups who recounted many stories of horrible abuses and deaths. Labor unions and manufacturers also called the practice unfair because they could not compete with those who used the cheap prisoner labor. In 1886 manufacturers organized the National Anti–Convict Contract Association and lobbied Congress to pass laws prohibiting the use of convict labor.

However, it was one man, George Washington Cable, a newspaper reporter from New Orleans, who brought the contract system to the attention of the American public. In a series of articles in the early 1880s, Cable revealed the system for what it was: "It kills like a pestilence, teaches the people to be cruel, sets up a false system of clemency, and seduces the State into the committal of murder for money," he wrote.

The practice of leasing out convict labor to private contractors eventually undermined the federal government's arrangements with state prisons and necessitated the creation of a federal prison system.

In 1887 Congress prohibited contracting the labor of federal prisoners, mainly because of pressure from the labor unions and manufacturers' lobbyists. Although several states soon passed similar laws, most other states reacted by simply refusing to accept federal prisoners. As a result, many federal prisoners now had to be transported long distances to serve their sentences. For example, prisoners from the Utah and Wyoming territories were taken to Jackson, Michigan.

Pressure mounted for the federal government to build and run its own prisons. Finally, in 1891, Congress authorized construction of three prisons under the direction of the Department of Justice: one in the North, one in the South, and one west of the Rocky Mountains. However, no money was appropriated for their construction. So instead of building a prison, the government borrowed one.

A military prison at an army base near Leavenworth, Kansas, a few miles north of Kansas City, was chosen for the first federal prison. On July 1, 1895, Congress transferred ownership of the prison from the army to the Department of Justice. The prison was hopelessly antiquated, however. The cell buildings had wooden floors, stairs, and ceilings. Each cellblock of 40 to 90 cells had only one door. There was great danger of a fire that would claim many lives. Perhaps the threat of such a scandal prompted Congress to act. On June 10, 1896, Congress authorized a new penitentiary to be constructed on a remote section of the same army base.

In the spring of 1897 construction was begun with convict labor. It was a massive project for the prisoners, most of whom were unskilled laborers. Each day 60 or more prisoners worked as stone cutters, about 200 as excavators, and about 130 as simple laborers. Much of the day was spent marching the prisoners to and from the work site three miles away. The main building was 800 feet long, with 1,200 cells built in the Auburn, congregate style. By 1903 enough of the new prison had

Leavenworth, built with convict labor between 1897 and 1928, was the nation's first federal penitentiary.

been finished to allow some of the prisoners to move to the new facility. On February 1, 1906, the remaining prisoners moved to the new facility, and the dilapidated old firetrap was returned to the army. All of the cell-blocks were completed in 1919, and the workshops and administration building were completed by 1928. Construction of the prison had taken more than 25 years.

Long before completion the prison, designed for 1,200 cells, was hopelessly overcrowded. By 1910 the prisoner count was over 1,000; by 1920 it had more than doubled. A second massive federal prison was constructed at Atlanta, Georgia, opening for 350 prisoners in 1902; the prison, like Leavenworth, was designed for 1,200 cells. Its completion also took another 20 years. A third federal prison was established at a former territorial prison on McNeil Island, Washington, in Puget Sound. It opened in 1909.

Over the next few decades, federal penitentiaries led the way in reforming prison conditions, although the federal system was still a patchwork of institutions that were funded separately and run according to policies and procedures established by each warden. In Atlanta, Warden William H. Moyer removed the benches in the dining room that had forced all prisoners to eat facing another man's back and installed tables and chairs. He allowed talking at meals for the first time in 1912. He added a dentist and an oculist to the prison medical staff. He instituted daily calisthenics and organized a 30-piece prison orchestra that played at

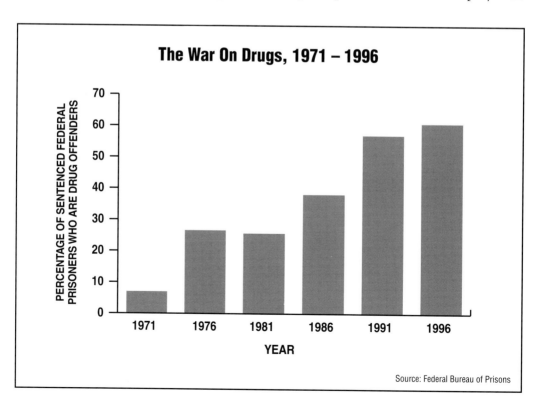

The War On Drugs, 1971 – 1996

Source: Federal Bureau of Prisons

mealtimes. He opened a prison school and began a baseball program that included several teams. A federal women's prison, opened in Alderson, West Virginia, in 1928, had no surrounding fences, and the prisoners were housed in cottages decorated with curtains.

However, the most sweeping and lasting reforms initiated by the federal prison system came after Congress established the Federal Bureau of Prisons (BOP) in 1930. The bureau's mission was to oversee all of the federal prisons throughout the country (at the time there were seven), and to this end it developed a comprehensive system of prisoner classification. For the first time, low-risk offenders and more-hardened criminals were separated and sent to different kinds of prisons so that, in the language of the bureau, "the individual needs of offenders" could be better met.

The BOP's first director, Sanford Bates, initiated

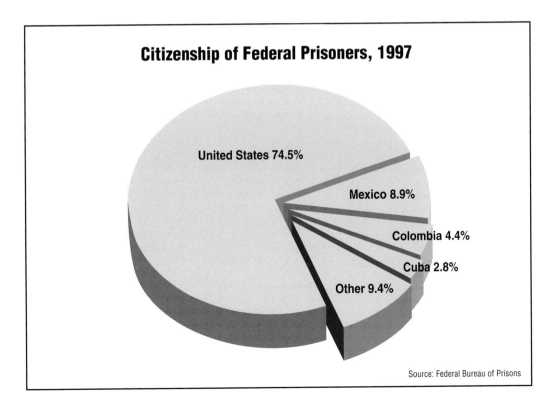

Citizenship of Federal Prisoners, 1997

United States 74.5%

Mexico 8.9%

Colombia 4.4%

Cuba 2.8%

Other 9.4%

Source: Federal Bureau of Prisons

another important administrative change: whereas previously the job of federal warden was bestowed as a political favor, it was now earned through the merit system of civil service. In addition, all new wardens were trained at a BOP school.

In 1937 the BOP brought all of its jobs within the prison system under the umbrella of the Federal Civil Service. This increased wages and prestige for the guards and established uniform standards of guard behavior throughout the federal prison system. When a guard received a promotion, he was transferred to another prison to prevent favoritism among the staff of any one prison.

The BOP also established, in 1934, an ambitious prison industries program, called Federal Prison Industries, Inc. (now also known by the trade name UNI-COR). Over the years, this government corporation has employed tens of thousands of federal prisoners in a chain of manufacturing plants. Currently, about one-quarter of all federal prisoners work in the program. The goods produced, which range from office furniture to electronic cable assemblies to combat helmets, are sold to other government agencies, and the profit is used to fund other BOP programs. The inmates are paid a small wage.

Mainly because of these and other programs and administrative reforms, after the establishment of the BOP, the federal prisons quickly earned the reputation among criminals as the best-run prisons in the country.

For the nation's most dangerous criminals, however, a maximum-security classification in the federal prison system meant spartan living conditions and slim possibilities for escape. In 1934 Alcatraz, the prison of last resort for only the most "vicious and irredeemable type," was opened on an island in San Francisco Bay. The federal government took several hundred of the most notorious crooks of the era—Al Capone and Baby Face Nelson included—and put them on "the Rock."

Prisoners there received almost no privileges, conversation between inmates was severely limited, and all mail from the outside was recopied onto prison stationery to prevent smuggling and to keep secret messages from reaching the prisoners. Unlike other prisons, Alcatraz was never allowed to become overcrowded. By the time it closed in 1963, it had housed only 1,557 prisoners in its 30-year history; at any one time, there were never more than 302 prisoners there.

It is a popular myth that no one ever escaped from Alcatraz. Over the years, several dozen men actually did escape from their cells. But all those who got off the island disappeared without a trace, and their bodies were never found. The authorities presumed that all died by drowning in their attempt to reach the mainland by swimming across San Francisco Bay, which has extremely treacherous currents and cold water.

Today the BOP operates 91 facilities, including penitentiaries, federal correctional institutions, federal prison camps, and federal medical centers for seriously ill inmates. It also contracts with community corrections centers and detention facilities to house federal prisoners on a per capita basis.

As of August 1997 the federal prisoner population was 111,135, with just over 100,000 in BOP facilities. Of those inmates, almost 93 percent were male, and more than 60 percent were sentenced for drug offenses (compared with, for example, just 2.5 percent sentenced for violent offenses). With the nation's "war on drugs," the number of federal inmates serving time for drug offenses has risen steadily since the early 1980s— a situation mirrored in state prisons. In large measure because of the drug trade, about 20 percent of the federal prison population consists of non-U.S. citizens: in August 1997, for example, some 8.9 percent of federal prisoners were Mexicans, and another 4.4 percent were Colombians.

REFORMS
AND RIOTS

By the 1940s the reforms pioneered by the Federal Bureau of Prisons had begun to spread to the majority of state prison systems. Corporal punishment, which had long served as the ultimate means by which prison administrators maintained control, largely disappeared. Prisoners who presented disciplinary problems were managed by solitary confinement, or what penologists today call administrative segregation. The code of silence that had been an integral feature of the Auburn system also was jettisoned, and prisoners now were allowed to talk and mingle freely in the exercise yard and dining hall.

In the postwar period crime was low, prisons were relatively inexpensive to run, and, most important, America's penal system seemed to be working. In 1950 state and federal penitentiaries held 166,000 prisoners, a drop of 8,000 from 1940. In 1946 the murder rate was 6.9 per 100,000 persons; in 1962 it was 4.5 per 100,000, a one-third decrease. Average citizens worried little

Attica uprising, September 10, 1971: Inmates demanding improvements in their living conditions occupy the prison yard. Three days later authorities would move against the rioters with a massive and deadly assault.

about prisons. Lawmakers and prison administrators felt that their primary goal—the rehabilitation of criminals into lawful citizens—was largely being met.

The prisoner-classification process that was begun by the federal Bureau of Prisons was expanded to include the advice of psychologists, case workers, sociologists, vocational counselors, and psychiatrists. It was a time when new prisons were built without the high walls and massive gray cellblocks of the traditional Big House. The men's prison at Soledad, California, was the first constructed after World War II. It contained cellblocks with day rooms and outside windows. Interior walls were painted in pastel colors. Large libraries and exercise facilities were included on the grounds. Discipline was relaxed, and a wide array of vocational training and group counseling was available for the inmates. In the 1960s at the Chino Prison in California, inmates lived in small units, each with an in-house counselor.

The Purposes of Prison

Historically, the rationales for imprisoning lawbreakers have varied from one society to another and have frequently changed over time within the same society. In the United States today, the debate about the purposes of imprisonment is dominated by four major arguments: retribution, incapacitation, deterrence, and rehabilitation.

Retribution is punishment. It is the infliction upon a criminal of what is judged to be a fair measure of pain in payment for the damage the criminal has done to society as a whole and to his or her particular victims. Society inflicts this pain by taking away the lawbreaker's freedom for a period of time, because in committing crimes the criminal misused his or her freedom. To those who believe that retribution is imprisonment's primary function—and, in a society as fed up with crime as is contemporary America, they are many—justice cannot be served unless criminals are made to suffer for their actions.

Incapacitation means simply that, while in prison, a criminal cannot commit any more crimes against society. He or she has been removed from our midst, so we are all safer. Several researchers have attempted to quantify the benefits of incapacitation. Their findings have varied considerably. For example, economist Edwin Zedlewski estimated, in a 1987 report for the National Institute of Justice, that the typical felon commits 187 crimes per year; in an article published in 1988, penologists Franklin E. Zimring and Gordon Hawkins dismissed that figure, saying the real number is closer to 20. Whatever

In 1954 the American Prison Association changed its name to the American Correctional Association. It urged members to refer to prisons as "correctional institutions" and punishment blocks within them as "adjustment centers."

But the confidence of the public and the self-satisfied attitude of many corrections professionals, as reflected by the new euphemisms, masked real conditions. A series of over 40 prison riots between 1952 and 1954 did little to change this complacent attitude. When officials investigated a prison riot at Jackson, Michigan, for example, they interviewed guards and administrative officers but not rioters. Prison riots became commonplace; in the United States there were more than 100 between 1954 and 1971.

In September 1971 the perception that America's prisons were a model of efficient management was shattered at New York's Attica Correctional Facility as

the case, to an American public that in recent years has expressed a widespread fear of violent crime, incapacitation seems a powerful reason for locking offenders up.

At present the argument for imprisonment as deterrence is less widely accepted than are the retribution or incapacitation rationales. The theory behind deterrence is that someone contemplating a crime will think twice if he or she knows that the consequences of being caught and convicted will be a prison sentence, especially a long one. For a percentage of potential criminals, the risk simply will not be worth it. Skeptics wonder whether the typical offender really considers the likelihood of getting caught. And anyway, the average felony sentence isn't terribly long—in 1994 in state court it was six years, with two years the average time actually served. But the most convincing argument against deterrence may be the nation's crime rate, which remains high despite the largest prisoner population in American history.

Rehabilitation—restoring the convict to a virtuous, productive life—once was seen as both the proper mission of the prison and as an attainable goal. No more. Although certain prison programs have reported success in lowering the recidivism (reoffending) rate of criminals, for the most part successes have been limited to low-level offenders. Of the approximately 400,000 convicts released from American prisons each year, 40 percent will be back behind bars within three years.

Americans saw traumatic images from an unfolding crisis on television. The situation began when prisoners seized a cellblock and its exercise yard, killing two prison staffers and taking dozens of others hostage. As many as 1,500 of Attica's 2,237 inmates eventually joined in the uprising. Authorities had recently cut inmate programs, and the prisoners were demanding changes in the conditions of their confinement.

After four days of fruitless negotiations for the release of the hostages, authorities decided to retake control of Attica by force. On the morning of September 13, more than 1,000 heavily armed prison guards, state troopers, and sheriff's deputies stormed the prisoners' stronghold. When the fighting was over, 9 hostages and 32 prisoners were dead.

It would be difficult to overestimate the shock that Attica produced. Previously, if they thought about the subject at all, Americans had largely assumed that their prisons were secure, competently and humanely administered, and at least somewhat successful at rehabilitating inmates. How could the inmates have taken over the prison? And what explained the depth of their bitterness?

In the wake of the carnage, a commission was established to study what had gone wrong at Attica. In its official report, the McKay Commission pointed a finger at decisions to cut educational and recreational opportunities for the inmates. But while the slashing of programs, in combination with increasingly restrictive rules that the commission said had also been enacted, may go a long way toward explaining why the prisoners rebelled, it does not explain how authorities lost control of the prison. That question is more complicated—and the answer, ultimately, more problematic.

Cumulatively, the penal reforms undertaken since the early 19th century—reforms designed to make incarceration more humane, rehabilitation more likely, and prison administration more economical—have had

another, unintended effect: they have gradually shifted control of prisons away from prison staff. Control was not an issue at Philadelphia's Cherry Hill Penitentiary; there, each inmate had his own cell with his own walled yard and was kept completely isolated from other inmates. With the rise of the Auburn-style prison, many inmates were housed together in smaller spaces. But while they worked and ate together, a strict code of silence and severe corporal punishment for rules violations ensured that discipline would be maintained. With the elimination of codes of silence and corporal punishment, along with the allowance of prisoner interaction in the exercise yard and at various free times during the day, the potential for prisoner violence and rebellion was vastly increased. One solution that many prison administrators turned to was the so-called con-boss system, by which a designated inmate—typically the toughest—was given special privileges in return for controlling the other inmates on

California's Soledad, the first American prison constructed after World War II. With day rooms, pastel colors, outside windows, and attractive grounds, it reflected penologists' confidence in the efficacy of rehabilitative treatment. That confidence would be rocked by a succession of prison riots and undermined by a growing public clamor for harsh punishment.

his cellblock and alerting guards to potential danger. When this arrangement fell out of favor as the result of widespread abuses, prison guards were left with dramatically less coercive power. (This issue is discussed further in the next chapter.)

In 1972, a year after the Attica violence, prison riots nationwide grew to an average of four per month. As the 1970s progressed, traditional views toward crime and punishment were increasingly questioned. Many people began to view the rehabilitative ideal, the idea that criminals could be "treated" and made into law-abiding citizens, as a fantasy. Others believed simply that current prison practices weren't serving the goal of rehabilitation well. The McKay Commission's assessment of conditions at Attica sounded a warning about correctional institutions throughout the country. It was likely, the commission stated, that the majority of inmates would leave prison "more embittered, more anti-social, and more prone to violence than they were when they entered."

By the late 1970s rising crime rates and a growing fear of violent crime had spurred widespread sentiment for punishing criminals severely, and legislatures began to take action toward that end. Gone was the old Quaker view of wrongdoers as "lost brethren"; Americans were tired of crime and palpably angry at criminals. They wanted the justice system to stop "coddling" lawbreakers, which meant longer prison sentences and an end to what were seen as easy conditions of confinement. This attitude has endured to the present, if anything becoming more entrenched over the years.

But a particularly brutal prison uprising in 1980 seemed to underscore the limits of "warehousing" criminals. At the New Mexico State Penitentiary in Santa Fe, a two-day riot that ended on February 3 caused $40 million in property damage and left 33 prisoners dead. Many had been raped, tortured, and mutilated by fellow inmates.

In its report on the riot, the New Mexico Attorney General's office blamed increased restrictions on inmates and the elimination of "incentive controls"— programs that inmates could participate in as a reward for good behavior and from which they could be removed as punishment for misbehavior. It is precisely these programs that make prison life easier for inmates, which some Americans feel criminals don't deserve. But such programs, the report concluded, are indispensable. For without "a certain degree of voluntary compliance that is largely gained by giving inmates a self interest in maintaining orderly behavior," prison officials cannot hope to maintain their tenuous hold:

> We can only stay in control of prisons to the degree that the prison population as a whole sees our administration as fair, human, somewhat reasonable, something they can understand. When we reach the point where a large number of prisoners see our administration as something other than that, then we have the potential for anything. The walls, the bars, the sallyports and all the impressive clanging hardware are deceptive in their promise of security.

With a pair of inmates lying nearby, National Guardsmen maintain a perimeter in the yard of the New Mexico State Penitentiary after a two-day rampage by prisoners. An official report on the February 1980 prison riot blamed the elimination of incentive programs that gave inmates a self-interest in orderly behavior.

ABOVE WHAT IS AUTHORIZED BY LAW?

Loss of freedom is the penalty criminals pay for breaking the law. Other deprivations they might suffer while behind bars, a federal judge ruled in 1980, constitute "punishment above what is authorized by law."

In 1954 the Supreme Court of the United States ruled, in the case of *Brown v. Board of Education*, that the practice of maintaining separate public schools for white and black children violated the Constitution. Not only did the landmark decision jump-start the civil rights movement by which African Americans tore down the walls of official segregation; it also inspired other minority groups to mount legal challenges to the treatment they received. In 1966, for example, the courts recognized the constitutionally protected rights of mental patients to humane treatment. Four years later the Supreme Court ruled that poor people had a constitutionally protected right to welfare benefits.

Historically, prisoners did not often petition the courts because their legal access to the courts was rather limited. Prisoners in the United States have always had the right to challenge the facts of the criminal case that resulted in their imprisonment. This right is called habeas corpus, from the Latin meaning "you should have the body" (to prove a crime was committed), and it was guaranteed in the original text of the Constitution of 1787. In Article I, Section 9, the Constitution states:

> The Privilege of the Writ of Habeas Corpus shall not be suspended, unless when in Cases of Rebellion or Invasion the public Safety may require it.

Once sent to prison, however, a person experienced a "civil death"—in other words, he or she forfeited the civil rights guaranteed to citizens by the Constitution. The Thirteenth Amendment, ratified in 1865, declared,

> Neither slavery nor involuntary servitude, except as a punishment for crime whereof the party shall have been duly convicted, shall exist within the United States, or any place subject to their jurisdiction.

Ironically, this amendment, which abolished the institution of black slavery, permitted the imposition of slavery upon convicts. Many states followed the example of the Thirteenth Amendment and passed laws that not only openly declared convicts slaves of the state, but also removed them from legal status in matters of their property, their marriage, and the welfare and custody of their children. Their treatment, good or ill, was left to the discretion—or whim—of the warden and staff of the institution in which they were incarcerated. The only constitutional limitation on the treatment of prisoners was found in the Eighth Amendment, which prohibits the infliction of "cruel and unusual punishments." That phrase, however, is somewhat vague, and as the Supreme Court stated in a 1958 decision, the Eighth Amendment "must draw its meaning from the evolving standards of decency that mark the progress of a maturing society." In other words, a punishment that was considered acceptable 100, 50, or even 25 years ago might today be considered cruel and unusual.

Early Eighth Amendment challenges from prisoners

centered on specific punishments. *In re Kemmler*, a case decided by the Supreme Court in 1890, is a good example. William Kemmler, of Buffalo, New York, had been sentenced to die for the murder of his girlfriend. The execution was to be carried out by means of the newly invented electric chair, which Kemmler maintained would constitute cruel and unusual punishment. The Supreme Court disagreed, and Kemmler became the first convict to die in the electric chair.

Later, the Eighth Amendment's prohibition of cruel and unusual punishment was applied not simply to physical punishments per se but also to conditions that existed within prisons—conditions that often were not, strictly speaking, intended as part of the sentence convicts received in punishment for their crimes. (A more detailed discussion of what the Supreme Court has said are unconstitutional conditions of confinement comes in the next chapter.)

Until the 1940s prisoners were generally allowed to petition the courts only on matters first approved by prison administrators. Then an important court decision, *Coffin v. Reichard*, upheld the right of prisoners to complain in federal court about the violation of civil rights that they still retained in state prison. By this decision, convicts were given the chance to submit legal petitions to the courts regardless of the local prison's policy. What actual rights the prisoner retained, however, would have to be decided on a case-by-case basis.

In 1962 Thomas Cooper, a Black Muslim leader in Stateville Prison in Illinois, submitted a petition claiming that Warden Pate denied Muslims the freedom of religion that was guaranteed to all by the Constitution. Muslims inside the prison were not allowed the Koran and other Muslim literature and were denied access to their clergy, though Jewish and Christian prisoners were afforded the facilities to practice their religion. Cooper claimed that he and all the Black Muslim convicts in the prison were being denied their rights under Section 1983 of the Civil Rights Act of 1871. That law, which was enacted to combat the practice of lynchings by the Klu Klux Klan, stated,

> Every person, who, under color of any statute, ordinance, regulation, custom or usage, of any State or Territory . . . subjects, or causes to be subject, any citizen of the United States or other person within the jurisdiction thereof to the deprivation of any rights, privileges, or immunities secured by the Constitution and laws, shall be liable to the party injured in an action at law, suit in equity, or other proper proceeding for redress.

Section 1983 became an important tool of the civil rights movement in attacking segregation, and it became just as important to inmates who wanted to

Prison Security Classifications

Generalizing about "the prison experience" is difficult not only because administrative practices and culture vary from institution to institution but also because different prisons are designed to house different types of offenders. Minimum-security prisons, which hold only the most trustworthy inmates who have no history of violence, typically have no armed guards and sometimes even no walls. Prisoners live in small, private rooms or in dorms and get liberal visitation privileges, leading some observers to wonder where the punishment lies. For example, the amenities at Allenwood, a minimum-security federal prison in Pennsylvania, earned it the nickname "Club Fed."

Medium-security institutions house inmates whose criminal records might include some violence but who are nevertheless viewed as good candidates for reintegration into society. For this reason, these prisons tend to emphasize programs designed to treat offenders, and their visitation policies may be fairly liberal. They do, however, have fences and armed guards.

Maximum-security prisons house the most dangerous and violent offenders. The primary focus of these institutions—preventing escape—is evident in their characteristic design, which includes guard towers, high walls topped with razor wire, and multiple fences. Visitor contact tends to be closely supervised and strictly limited, and rehabilitation efforts and educational opportunities may be minimal. At the extreme end of the maximum-security classification is the federal prison in Marion, Illinois, where the most dangerous federal prisoners are held, one per cell, with virtually no contact with fellow inmates. Inmates under administrative segregation at Marion leave their cells for only a half hour per day, to shower and take 20 minutes of solitary exercise.

force prison administrators to change conditions and practices in their penitentiaries.

This minimum-security facility in Vienna, Illinois, looks more like a townhouse complex than a prison.

In Texas a convicted thief named David Ruiz used Section 1983 to challenge the conditions of his confinement. Ruiz, who had stabbed several other inmates during his time in the Texas Department of Corrections' Eastham Unit, was frequently placed in solitary confinement. In a 30-page, handwritten petition that he submitted to Eastham's warden, Billy McMillan, Ruiz claimed that conditions in solitary confinement were inhumane. He also said that the practice of using convicts as guards was unconstitutional.

For about a decade the Texas Department of Corrections had allowed selected convicts, called hall janitors or building tenders, to live in unlocked cells and receive better food and job assignments in return for turning cell doors, doing prisoner counts, and maintaining order on their cellblock tiers. It was a variation of the old con-boss arrangement. The building tender system seemed to make sense for a prison system trying to run its institutions in the most economical fashion: order could be maintained with the fewest guards. On weekends, one prison's staff consisted of just 12 officers; the building tenders performed virtually all the necessary functions.

Not surprisingly, building tenders came from the ranks of the prison's toughest inmates. Jerry Ray Bolden, building tender of the Eastham Unit wing where the most dangerous prisoners were kept, described what it took to do his job:

> You can't control people who consider themselves gangsters by word of mouth. You let them know every day who's running the tank—whatever it took to convince them. You don't say, "Would you please do this? . . . You need a certain amount of force, a certain amount of fear and a certain amount of respect.

With building tenders who were not only tough but also predatory, the system could easily lead to significant abuses.

When David Ruiz submitted his first petition to Billy McMillan, the warden wasn't too receptive. Ruiz later described what happened:

> You know what he did? He said, "I'm going to tell you what I think about inmates' rights . . . This." And he tore it in half. So I drafted another one.

Ruiz's perseverance was rewarded on June 29, 1972, when his fourth petition reached the desk of Judge William Wayne Justice of the Eastern District Court. Judge Justice, who had been appointed to the federal bench by President Lyndon Johnson, had earned a reputation for judicial activism.

His activism was evidenced in the case of *Ruiz v. Estelle,* which began in 1972 and dragged on for a decade. In 1974 Justice gathered seven similar petitions from other inmates of Texas prisons and fashioned a class action lawsuit—a suit filed by one or more plaintiffs on behalf of themselves as well as all other persons identically wronged—that alleged a consistent pattern of unconstitutional abuse of prisoners' rights. He even brought under his review issues that the inmate plaintiffs had not raised—for example, prison crowding, recreational facilities, and prison land use. Ultimately, every aspect of the way Texas ran its prisons came under scrutiny, and the assumption, one of Justice's aides later revealed, was that the Texas Department of Corrections was "rotten from top to bottom, that everything had to change."

Justice appointed William Bennett Turner, a lawyer for the National Association for the Advancement of Colored People (NAACP), to head the plaintiffs' legal team and persuaded the U.S. Department of Justice to act on the side of the convicts as well. The actual trial, which lasted 159 days, began in 1978. In his 188-page decision, delivered in 1980, Justice declared the Texas prison system an affront to civilized society. "The incarceration is punishment, the rest is punishment above what is authorized by law," he stated in ordering a comprehensive overhaul of the system.

Court-ordered walk: Texas inmates at the Walls Unit in Huntsville enjoy early releases because of prison overcrowding.

Some of the changes Justice ordered were general (better medical care, more guards, fairer procedures for dealing with inmate grievances). Others, however—like housing one inmate per cell, eliminating the building tender system, changing the prisoner classification system so that fewer inmates would be designated maximum security, and dividing the prisoner population into 500-person management units—involved the details of daily prison management. Without exception, the major issues of *Ruiz v. Estelle* were decided in favor of the prisoners.

The Texas Department of Corrections appealed, maintaining that the changes Justice had ordered would cause a massive breakdown in prison discipline and lead to violence. Although the U.S. Circuit Court of Appeals for the Fifth District did overturn some provisions of Judge Justice's order, it essentially accepted his finding that on the whole, conditions in Texas state prisons were cruel and unusual and hence unconstitutional. The Texas Department of Corrections would have to change the way it operated.

By most assessments the results were disastrous. Whatever else might be said about the Texas prison system before *Ruiz*—and there is no denying that its disciplinary policies were strict—its facilities were safe, with assault rates far below the national average. And it had the nation's only fully accredited prison educational system; it operated a huge, profitable system of prisoner-worked farms; and its costs per inmate were the lowest in the country.

After *Ruiz*, the prisons' educational and agricultural programs fell apart and costs per inmate soared. But most horribly, with the dismantling of the building tender system, the mandated reduction in maximum-security designations, and other changes, Texas prisons experienced a nightmarish wave of violence. In 1984 and 1985 there were 52 murders, more than 600 stabbings, and 80,000 incidents of prisoner misconduct. During one week alone—August 31 to September 9, 1985—eight Texas prisoners were murdered. Rape became widespread. White, black, and Latino prison gangs organized to protect themselves, extort favors from others, and conduct criminal enterprises both inside and outside the prisons.

"There are more bosses [guards] now," observed former Eastham building tender Jerry Ray Bolden, "but so many are inexperienced and young. So many are scared, so many don't know how to stop certain situations. The inmates know there's no one there."

Gary Gomez, a veteran Eastham guard, echoed Bolden's assessment. "All of a sudden," he said, "we realized we didn't have control. We had some liberal judge telling us how to run a penitentiary, and he's never worked inside a pen."

Historically, American judges had been reluctant to tell prison officials how to run their penitentiaries. A 1954 federal circuit court ruling declared that judges "are without power to direct prison administration or to interfere with ordinary prison rules and regulations." But beginning in the early 1970s, that changed. The case of *Ruiz v. Estelle*, which transformed the nation's largest prison system, found echoes in other court cases in other states, though the results weren't often as dramatic. Nevertheless, by 1986 a total of 33 states operated their prisons under federal court orders. In many instances judicial mandates to relieve prison overcrowding took the form of caps on prison populations, and authorities whose institutions exceeded those caps were forced to release convicts early or to find alternatives to incarceration.

The cost of mandated prison reforms for overcrowded conditions at that time was about $70,000 a cell. The state of Texas alone spent over $1 billion to comply with the various court-ordered reforms to its prison facilities.

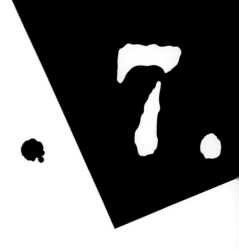

SUBJECT TO SCRUTINY

What rights do prisoners have, and when do prison conditions violate the Constitution's ban on cruel and unusual punishment? The Supreme Court has wrestled with these questions in a succession of important cases.

While lower courts made large-scale interventions in prison systems across the country to correct conditions of confinement they deemed unconstitutional under the Eighth Amendment, the Supreme Court remained largely on the sidelines. Not until 1981, with the case of *Rhodes v. Chapman*, did the Court consider, in the words of Justice Lewis Powell, "a disputed contention that the conditions of confinement at a particular prison constituted cruel and unusual punishment." "Nor have we," Powell continued, "had an occasion to consider specifically the principles relevant to assessing claims that conditions of confinement violate the Eighth Amendment."

That is not to say that the Supreme Court didn't consider prison conditions an Eighth Amendment concern. In a 1978 case, *Hutto v. Finney*, the Court stated, "Confinement in prison . . . is a form of punishment subject to scrutiny under the Eighth Amendment standards." And, in dealing with a succession of cases involving the question of whether a specific punishment was cruel and unusual, the Court established precedents that would affect its later rulings on prison conditions. In the death penalty case *Gregg v. Georgia*, decided in 1976, the Court stated that even if it was not physically barbarous, a punishment that "involve[s] the unnecessary and wanton infliction of pain" violates the Eighth Amendment. The following year, in *Coker v. Georgia*, the Court decided that a person could not be executed for rape and kidnapping, ruling that if punishment is grossly disproportionate to the crime committed, it is cruel and unusual.

In the 1976 case of *Estelle v. Gamble*, the Court upheld prisoners' constitutional right to adequate health care—a right that the rest of society does not enjoy—because an "inmate must rely on prison authorities to treat his medical needs; if the authorities fail to do so, those needs will not be met." Thus, the Court ruled, "deliberate indifference to serious medical need" constitutes cruel and unusual punishment, as it can result in pain that serves no penological purpose or, in extreme cases, in physical torture. At the same time, however, the Court set the bar fairly high for proving a constitutional violation in such cases: something more than ordinary negligence was required.

The case of *Rhodes v. Chapman* began as a class action suit filed in federal district court by inmates at the Southern Ohio Correctional Facility. Authorities at that institution, a maximum-security state prison in Lucasville, had initiated "double celling"—housing two prisoners in cells that were designed to hold one—because of a sharp increase in Ohio's inmate population. The suit charged that double celling constituted cruel and unusual punishment and sought an injunction to stop the practice except as a temporary measure.

Opened in 1972, the Southern Ohio Correctional Facility was in many respects a model prison. It had a

25,000-volume library; dayrooms where inmates could socialize, watch TV, or play cards between 6:30 A.M. and 9:30 P.M.; gymnasiums, workshops, and classrooms; two chapels; and an outdoor garden, recreation field, and visitation area. Contact visitation (in which the prisoner and visitor are in the same room and may actually touch, rather than merely talking through a Plexiglas wall) was permitted for all inmates, a rarity in maximum-security prisons. Cells were well ventilated and had a sink with hot and cold running water, a bed, a toilet, a nightstand, and a cabinet, shelf, and radio built into the wall.

But the prison was housing 38 percent more inmates than its design capacity, and the 63 square feet that double-celled inmates shared fell well below the minimum standard for living space as defined by various organizations. (The American Public Health Associa-

An injured inmate is helped from an ambulance by hospital personnel. The 1976 Supreme Court case of Estelle v. Gamble *established prisoners' constitutional right to adequate health care—a right the rest of society does not automatically enjoy.*

tion and the Justice Department have given 60 square feet of living quarters per person as the minimum standard; some independent studies have put the figure as low as 50 square feet per person.)

The district court ruled that double celling at the Southern Ohio Correctional Facility was cruel and unusual punishment, declaring, "Overcrowding necessarily involves excess limitation of general movement as well as physical and mental injury from long exposure." It issued an injunction ordering prison officials to end the practice.

The Court of Appeals for the Sixth Circuit upheld the ruling, and when Ohio officials appealed again, the Supreme Court agreed to hear the case because of its implications for prison administration. In its decision, the Court emphasized that the principles it had enunciated in deciding such cases as *Gregg v. Georgia* and *Coker v. Georgia* "apply when the conditions of confinement compose the punishment at issue. Conditions must not involve the wanton and unnecessary infliction of pain, nor may they be grossly disproportionate to the severity of the crime warranting imprisonment." And pain that serves no penological purpose is unconstitutional. "But," the Court continued, "conditions that cannot be said to be cruel and unusual under contemporary standards are not unconstitutional. To the extent that such conditions are restrictive and even harsh, they are part of the penalty that criminal offenders pay for their offenses against society." Double celling at the Ohio facility had not led to "deprivations of essential food, medical care, or sanitation" or to an increase in violence, so there was no Eighth Amendment violation. "[T]he Constitution does not mandate comfortable prisons," the Court said, ending its decision overturning the ban on double celling with an admonishment to the lower courts to give legislatures and prison authorities latitude in making administrative decisions about how to run their prisons.

Prisoners at the Massachu-setts Correctional Institute in Concord (shown here) were forced to sleep in the infirmary after the inmate population swelled to nearly three times the prison's origi-nal capacity. Sharp rises in incarceration rates have caused many correctional facilities to become over-crowded, and while lower courts have frequently issued injunctions capping prison populations, the Supreme Court in Rhodes v. Chap-man declared that "the Constitution does not man-date comfortable prisons."

In several subsequent cases the Supreme Court has reiterated the need for the courts to recognize the com-plexities of running a prison and to stop second-guess-ing prison authorities. *Whitley v. Albers* dealt with guards' use of force in resolving a prison disturbance at the Oregon State Penitentiary. On June 20, 1980, inmates in that prison's cellblock A, a two-tiered unit housing some 200 prisoners, took hostage a guard who was attempting to get them to return to their cells, and began breaking glass and furniture. The leader of the rioters was an inmate named Richard Klenk.

New Jersey state corrections officers in riot gear move to take control of the Hudson County Jail, January 1996. Whitley v. Albers gave prison authorities wide latitude in dealing with prison disturbances.

The prison's security manager, Captain Harold Whitley, entered cellblock A to evaluate the situation. He spoke with Klenk and was taken to see the captured guard. The hostage was in an upper-tier cell, along with several inmates who assured Whitley that they would protect him from any other prisoners who tried to harm him. Klenk, however, informed Whitley that he would kill the guard if an attempt was made to retake the cellblock by force; he had a knife, and other inmates were armed with homemade clubs. As he was leaving cellblock A, Whitley was approached by an inmate named Gerald Albers, who was not involved in the disturbance. (Whitley later said he didn't recall speaking to Albers.) Albers asked the security manager for the key to a row of lower-tier cells that housed elderly and sick prisoners; he wanted to get these men out of harm's way in case tear gas was used. Whitley said he would return with the key.

After he left the cellblock, Whitley organized a squad of guards to quell the disturbance. The plan was for Whitley, unarmed, to enter cellblock A first; he would proceed up the stairs to the second tier to obtain the release of the hostage. Close behind Whitley would be two officers armed with shotguns, followed by a wave of officers without guns. Whitley directed the officers with shotguns to fire a warning shot as they entered the cellblock, then to shoot low at anyone who tried to follow him up the stairs, as these inmates might pose a threat to him and the hostage.

By the time the assault force was ready, more than a half hour after the guard was seized, the cellblock appeared to have quieted down, though a group of inmates still had not returned to their cells. When Whitley climbed over an inmate-erected barricade and entered the cellblock again, Albers asked him for the key to the elderly and sick prisoners' cells. The security manager said no, yelled "Shoot the bastards," then ran toward the steps, where Klenk was headed. As Whitley chased Klenk up the stairs, the officers with shotguns entered and fired a warning shot. When Albers—in what he later said was an attempt to return to his cell—ran up the stairs also, one of the officers shot him in the knee. Whitley, meanwhile, managed to subdue Klenk and free the unharmed hostage.

Albers brought an action in federal district court against Whitley, the guard who shot him, and other prison officials, claiming that they had violated his Eighth Amendment rights. The cellblock disturbance had subsided by the time the guards entered; officers had failed to issue a verbal warning before firing; and Whitley knew Albers wasn't one of the rioters anyway. Thus, in using deadly force against him, the officers had acted with "deliberate indifference" to his rights, Albers maintained.

The district court decided that Albers hadn't presented evidence compelling enough to warrant consideration of the case by a jury, but on appeal this decision was overturned, and the case was eventually argued before the Supreme Court on December 10, 1985. In a 5-4 decision handed down on March 4 of the following year, the Court sided with Whitley et al. "To be cruel and unusual punishment," the majority declared, "conduct that does not purport to be punishment at all must involve more than ordinary lack of due care for the prisoner's interests or safety." (By "conduct that does not purport to be punishment," the Court meant any act or omission by prison authorities that was not part of the prisoner's formal sentence handed down by a court or judge.) "It is obduracy and wantonness," the Court stated,

> not inadvertence or error in good faith, that characterize the conduct prohibited by the Cruel and Unusual Punishments Clause, whether that conduct occurs in connection with establishing conditions of confinement, supplying medical needs, or restoring control over a tumultuous cellblock. The infliction of pain in the course of a prison security measure, therefore, does not amount to cruel and unusual punishment simply because it may appear in retrospect that the degree of force authorized or applied for security purposes was unreasonable, and hence unnecessary in the strict sense.

The "deliberate indifference" standard applied in *Estelle*, the Court found, is not applicable in cases involving prison disturbances, during which decisions must be "made in haste, under pressure, and frequently without the luxury of a second chance." Furthermore, dealing with a prison riot is unlike providing medical services because it involves competing obligations: ensuring the safety of prison staff and nonrioting inmates and minimizing harm to rioters. Citing a previously decided case, the Court said that the yardstick for determining whether prison authorities had acted unconstitutionally during a prison disturbance is whether their actions were undertaken "maliciously and sadistically for the very purpose of causing harm."

Whitley v. Albers would figure in another prisoners' rights case, *Wilson v. Seiter,* decided in 1991. Pearly L. Wilson, a felon, claimed that conditions of confinement at the Hocking Correctional Facility in Nelsonville, Ohio, where he was incarcerated, violated his Eighth Amendment rights. Among the conditions he cited were overcrowding; inadequate heating, cooling, and ventilation; unsanitary dining facilities and food preparation; and the housing of healthy inmates with mentally and physically ill inmates. He sought an injunction to remedy these conditions as well as $900,000 in damages.

The Supreme Court's *Rhodes v. Chapman* and *Whitley v. Albers* decisions had established two hurdles that prisoners seeking to prove Eighth Amendment violations had to clear. Rhodes was a more objective one: was the deprivation a prisoner suffered sufficiently

Inmate food handlers assemble a meal. Unsanitary dining facilities and food preparation have been among the conditions prisoners have cited in lawsuits alleging violations of their Eighth Amendment rights.

serious? If not, there could be no cruel and unusual punishment. *Whitley* emphasized a subjective component: did prison authorities' actions stem from "malicious" or "sadistic" motives? Wilson's lawyers believed they had cleared the first hurdle. And they conceded that in certain instances, the state of mind of prison officials was crucial. If a heater broke down during a frigid winter, for example, that would produce a serious deprivation for prisoners, yet no one could blame prison officials for wantonly inflicting pain and suffering, and there would be no Eighth Amendment issue. But, Wilson's lawyers argued, when deplorable prison conditions persist over a long period of time, the state of mind of officials is irrelevant. Whatever the reason, the conditions are objectively cruel and unusual. Thus, they proposed distinguishing between "one-time" or "short-term" conditions (like a prison disturbance) and "continuing" or "systemic" conditions. With the former, a prisoner alleging cruel and unusual punishment would have to demonstrate that officials had acted with a culpable state of mind; with the latter, they would not.

The Court rejected this argument, saying,

> We perceive neither a logical nor a practical basis for that distinction. The source of the intent requirement is not the predilections of this Court, but the Eighth Amendment itself, which bans only cruel and unusual punishment. If the pain inflicted is not formally meted out by the statute or the sentencing judge, some mental element must be attributed to the inflicting officer before it can qualify. . . .
> . . . The long duration of a cruel prison condition may make it easier to establish knowledge, and hence some form of intent; but there is no logical reason why it should cause the requirement of intent to evaporate.

In a concurring opinion (an opinion that agrees with the decision but emphasizes a different approach) joined by Justices Marshall, Blackmun, and Stevens, Justice Byron White criticized the majority's reliance on intent to determine Eighth Amendment violations.

"In truth," he wrote, "intent simply is not very meaningful when considering a challenge to an institution, such as a prison system." White worried that the majority's approach might, for example, enable prison officials to stifle a challenge to "inhumane prison conditions simply by showing that the conditions are caused by insufficient funding from the state legislature, rather than by any deliberate indifference on the part of the prison officials."

The subjective test of intent fleshed out in *Wilson* was applied in the case of *Farmer v. Brennan*, decided on June 6, 1994. Dee Farmer, a male transsexual who had undergone operations to implant silicone breasts and to have his testicles removed, was serving a 20-year sentence for credit card fraud when federal prison officials transferred him from a correctional institution to a higher-security penitentiary and placed him in the general prison population. Farmer was subsequently beaten and raped by another inmate. Claiming that officials had acted with "deliberate indifference" to his safety even though he had never expressed his concerns to them, Farmer petitioned the courts for damages as well as an injunction prohibiting future confinement in any penitentiary. The crux of his case was that officials knew or should have known he would be attacked given his feminine characteristics and the history of inmate sexual assaults at the penitentiary. The Supreme Court rejected Farmer's argument:

> The [Eighth] Amendment outlaws cruel and unusual "punishments," not "conditions," and the failure to alleviate a significant risk that an official should have perceived but did not, while no cause for commendation, cannot be condemned as the infliction of punishment under the Court's cases.

This does not mean, the Court emphasized, that "prison officials will be free to ignore obvious dangers to inmates" or that inmates must wait to be harmed before they can get relief from the courts. It just means that

An inmate poses inside the library of a Utah state prison. The Supreme Court's 1977 Bounds v. Smith *decision mandated that states provide prisoners with the use of a law library or professional legal assistance to guarantee their right to "meaningful access" to the federal courts. Twenty years later, however, a more conservative Court dramatically limited states' obligations in* Lewis v. Casey.

inmates must demonstrate that officials knew of (or know of) the risk and failed to take reasonable action.

In unusually strong terms, Justice Harry Blackmun took exception to the majority's logic and to its *Wilson*-based intent requirements in a concurring opinion. "The responsibility for subminimal conditions in any prison," he declared,

> inevitably is diffuse, and often borne, at least in part, by the legislature. Yet regardless of what state actor or institution caused the harm and with what intent, the experience of the inmate is the same. A punishment is simply no less cruel or unusual because its harm is unintended. In view of this obvious fact, there is no reason to believe that, in adopting the Eighth Amendment, the Framers intended to prohibit cruel and unusual punishments only when they were inflicted intentionally.

Over the years, various specific prisoner rights have

been established. A convict in prison retains the rights of freedom of speech and religion. Prisoners are entitled to administrative due process—that is, they may not be punished for infractions committed inside prison unless they have been given a hearing to review the facts of the incident. And, of course, there is the more general right to be free from cruel and unusual punishment, which in effect amounts to a guarantee of a minimum standard of living. This includes adequate nutrition, medical care, sanitation, and measures to protect personal safety—although, as we have seen, recent Supreme Court decisions have placed upon inmates the burden of demonstrating that officials had a culpable state of mind in denying them these minimum standards.

Legal challenges to conditions of confinement are mounted every year, and we can expect the area of prisoners' rights to continue evolving under new court rulings. To a large extent, however, whatever power prisoners have to change the conditions under which they are confined or to obtain redress for violations of their constitutional rights depends on their ability to petition the federal courts. Without that ability, they would have to rely entirely on prison authorities to address their grievances.

In the case of *Bounds v. Smith*, decided in 1977, the Supreme Court affirmed the right of prisoners to "meaningful access to the Courts." Specifically, the Court said that "the fundamental constitutional right of access to the Courts requires prison authorities to assist inmates in the preparation and filing of meaningful legal papers by providing prisoners with adequate law libraries or adequate assistance from persons trained in the law."

The *Bounds* decision gave states the option of fulfilling their obligation through either a law library or legal assistance. But over the years, lower courts ruled that merely providing law books and journals might not be enough to guarantee meaningful access to the courts. How would a law library help illiterate or non-English-speaking prisoners, for example?

A recent case that gave the Supreme Court an opportunity to revisit the issue of "meaningful access" began in Arizona when 22 inmates filed a class action lawsuit alleging that the state's provisions for guaranteeing them access to the courts were constitutionally inadequate. The district court ruled in favor of the plaintiffs, and the United States Court of Appeals for the Ninth Circuit affirmed the decision.

Arizona was ordered to make a host of changes, some of which would be costly. For example, each prison library would have to be staffed by at least one full-time, professionally trained librarian with a library science, law, or paralegal degree, and each librarian would need secretarial support. Other prison-library staff members should have training in the rudiments of legal research because less than two-thirds of Arizona inmates can read above a seventh-grade level; bilingual law clerks were ordered because nearly 15 percent of Arizona's prisoners don't speak English. Library collections would have to be up-to-date and include specific publications. The libraries should be open at least 50 hours a week, and to bar certain inmates from physical access to the libraries, prison personnel were required to demonstrate that these inmates posed an actual security risk; even inmates under lockdown (confined to their cells for most of the day for security reasons) could not be routinely excluded. A videotaped course on legal research would have to be made available to all inmates; the course would have to be a minimum of 30 hours long. And all prisoners were entitled to three 20-minute calls to outside lawyers or legal organizations each week.

Unhappy with these court-mandated requirements, Arizona appealed the case, called *Lewis v. Casey*, to the U.S. Supreme Court. The state's attorney general argued that the earlier *Bounds* decision required only

Senator Orrin Hatch has been one of the most outspoken critics of prisoners' rights lawsuits.

that prisoners be "on a similar footing to those not incarcerated" in regard to their access to the courts, not that the state was required to help prisoners do thorough research and file effective legal briefs. In a 1996 article in *The New York Law Journal*, law professor Julius J. Marke summarized Arizona's arguments thusly: "[W]hy should prisoners get better legal assistance than most free citizens who cannot afford high-quality legal representation? The inability of a prisoner to do legal research is no more of a constitutional concern than of free citizens with a similar ineffectiveness."

When the Supreme Court delivered its decision in *Lewis v. Casey* on June 24, 1996, it sided with Arizona. The Court declared that prisoners have no right to a law library or legal assistance per se. Rather, they have the right only to access to the courts. And, the justices suggested, if the state made available forms upon which prisoners could write the facts of their cases and provided minimal legal advice, that might be sufficient. The "inordinately intrusive" order handed down by the lower court was unjustified, the Supreme Court said, because no pattern of "actual injury"—specifically, hampered ability of prisoners to file legitimate legal claims—was ever identified. Prisoners in the original class action suit had failed to demonstrate how alleged shortcomings in the law libraries had been detrimental to them *personally*, just as a healthy prisoner would be unable to show how inadequate medical facilities harmed him. More than an abstract or hypothetical injury is required, the Court ruled.

To numerous prison administrators, state attorneys general, and legislators, the *Lewis* ruling represents a step in the right direction. For too long, these and other critics charge, prisoners have been filing frivolous grievances under the guise of protecting their civil rights. "[W]e've gotten to the point," declared Senator Orrin Hatch of Utah, chairman of the Senate Judiciary Committee, "where prisoners' rights have almost taken precedence over everything else. . . . They're filing suits every day and clogging up the courts, and it is costing society a tremendous amount of money."

Twenty-one state attorneys general compiled a list of particularly irksome cases. These include: *Burton v. Kernan*, in which a prisoner said he suffered cruel and unusual punishment because he got a stomachache and diarrhea from eating prison chili; *Bittaker v. Rowland*, in which a prisoner claimed his rights were violated when he was served a soggy sandwich and a broken cookie; *Saddler v. Merkle*, in which a prisoner said he had suffered "mental anguish" worrying that guards would use tear gas to compel him to leave his cell; and *Garcia v. Rowland*, in which an inmate sued over prison officials' failure to give him five stamped envelopes (legal mail is supposed to be free for all prisoners).

Advocates for prisoners counter that for every frivolous lawsuit filed there are numerous cases of significant abuse by guards or serious negligence by prison authorities. Among the cases they cite are the following: *Madrid v. Gomez*, in which guards were found to have kicked, beaten, and scalded handcuffed and shackled prisoners; *Austin v. Department of Corrections*, in which more than 400 inmates of a single Pennsylvania prison became infected with tuberculosis after authorities ignored warnings from the Commissioner of Health; *Carson v. Seckinger*, in which guards, maintenance workers, and even a prison chaplain were found to have forced female inmates in Georgia to have sex with them; and *Yellen v. Ada County, Idaho*, in which jail officials negligently permitted a 17-year-old boy to be tortured for 14 hours and then murdered by cellmates who had only days earlier beaten another teenager unconscious.

In any event, prisoner lawsuits will likely decrease in the wake of the Supreme Court's *Lewis v. Casey* ruling and as a result of the Prisoner Litigation Reform Act, which was signed into law by President Clinton in April 1996. That act, which was designed to eliminate frivolous lawsuits, specifies that before prisoners file a suit, they must first exhaust all administrative channels to resolve their grievances. Any inmate who files three suits deemed frivolous is barred from future suits, with exceptions made only if the inmate is in imminent danger. The Prison Litigation Reform Act also limits both monetary awards to plaintiffs and attorneys' fees, presumably making these cases less attractive for lawyers.

8.

CAPTIVE NATION

erhaps the most striking aspect of the American criminal justice system today is the extraordinarily high rate of incarceration. Per capita, more people are incarcerated in the United States than in any other nation except Russia. And the rate has been increasing steadily for over a decade, more than doubling between 1985 and 1997.

According to the Bureau of Justice Statistics, a total of 744,208 inmates were held in state and federal prisons and local jails on December 31, 1985. By December 31, 1995, that number had skyrocketed to 1,585,401, a jump of 113 percent. By June 1996 it was 1,630,940; by June 1997, it stood at 1,725,842.

Another way to look at it is this: 1 in every 313 U.S. residents was behind bars at year-end 1985. At year-end 1995, that ratio stood at 1 in 167. By midyear 1997, the ratio was 1 in 155.

Close the door, turn the key: the solution to America's crime problem?

This staggering rate of incarceration has profound implications for all Americans, not just those who are serving time. The cost of feeding, housing, guarding, and treating America's prisoners presents a significant burden to taxpayers, especially in states where incarceration rates are highest. On June 30, 1994, it was estimated that each of the 980,513 inmates of state and federal prisons cost an average of $53.24 per day to maintain. The 490,442 men and women in the nation's 127 jail systems each cost an average of $46.97 every day. This means that in 1994 over $75 million was being spent every day just to keep the prisons and jails running, which works out to $27.375 billion annually. And this figure excludes not only the cost of running juvenile facilities but also the cost of court-mandated renovations to obsolete prison space and the cost of constructing new prisons to accommodate an ever-growing inmate population. These add billions more to the total. According to author Kathryn Watterson, who attempted to account for unreported costs such as guards' pensions, prisoner transportation, and hospitalization, the total bill for corrections in the United States in 1994 was actually over $85 billion. And the inmate population grew by 7.3 percent in 1995 and 4.4 percent in 1996.

These figures lead to some interesting questions: Why is America's incarceration rate so high, and why has it been increasing? Do the benefits of incarcerating so many offenders outweigh the costs? And what, if anything, could be done better?

Prison populations in the United States began growing in the early 1980s at a rate disproportionate to any increases in the number of crimes committed. The primary cause was a series of sentencing reform measures designed to stiffen penalties for society's most dangerous criminals. It was a time of widespread public fear of, and anger toward, violent criminals; a time when the illegal drug trade seemed especially insidious; and finally, a time when sentences for serious offenders seemed far too lenient. Consequently, it was a particu-

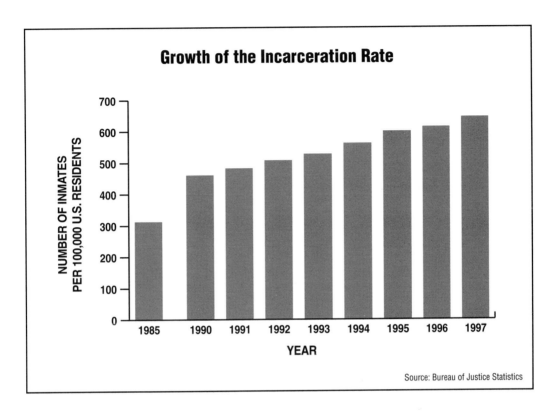

Growth of the Incarceration Rate

NUMBER OF INMATES PER 100,000 U.S. RESIDENTS

YEAR

Source: Bureau of Justice Statistics

larly good time for politicians to demonstrate that they were "tough on crime."

Whatever might be said about public fear of crime or the dangers of the drug trade, many researchers dispute the contention that criminal sentences in the United States were ever overly lenient. In their review "Crime Policy Report: Did Getting Tough on Crime Pay?", produced in August 1997 for The Urban Institute, William J. Sabol of The Urban Institute and James P. Lynch of American University write, "The misperception of leniency rested in large measure on erroneous or badly used data and on the media attention that focused on the unusual or atypically short sentences given to violent offenders."

Outrage over perceived lenient sentences for violent and so-called career criminals led to a more general belief that offenders of all types were getting off too eas-

America's incarceration rate, the second highest in the world, has increased steadily, more than doubling in just 12 years.

ily. And so, when sentencing reforms were enacted—for example, reforms that specified mandatory prison terms for certain offenses and mandatory minimum sentences—a large number of nonviolent, first-time, and drug offenders were incarcerated along with the violent and habitual criminals originally targeted. Particularly affected were drug users and low-level dealers, as more than 30 states passed mandatory-sentence laws for drug offenses and the federal government adopted a policy of "zero tolerance" of illegal drugs.

The zeal for incarceration has continued into the late 1990s, with various laws that are popularly referred to as "three strikes and you're out." Under these laws, a person receives a mandatory sentence of life imprisonment without the possibility of parole upon conviction of a third (usually violent) felony. On September 13, 1994, President Clinton signed the Violent Crime Control and Law Enforcement Act, which imposed a mandatory life sentence for those convicted of a third "serious violent felony" in federal court. Between 1993 and 1994 a total of 30 states passed similar laws for state offenders, and 10 other states have passed tougher laws for repeat offenders. "Violent felonies" include not only murder and rape, but also drug sales (federal), promoting prostitution (Washington), and burglary and selling drugs to minors (California).

Aside from greatly increasing the prison population, mandatory sentencing laws have had various unforeseen effects. In California, for example, the new laws have apparently led some judges who perceive them as unfair to change felony charges to misdemeanors so that a defendant won't be facing life in prison. Prosecutors also observe that plea bargaining in cases subject to the new sentencing mandates, particularly three-strikes-and-you're-out laws, has decreased sharply. Plea bargaining—a defendant's agreement to plead guilty to a lesser charge in return for a lesser sentence—is the way the overwhelming majority of criminal cases are

resolved. It spares both defendants and prosecutors the expense and uncertainty of a trial. And the simple fact is that prosecutors don't have the resources to try every case. But for a defendant subject to mandatory life imprisonment under three-strikes-and-you're-out rules, there's no incentive to plea-bargain. In 1993 the district attorney of Los Angeles County, Gil Garcetti, estimated that his office would need 40 new prosecutors and an additional $250 million a year because of the three-strikes law. Police officers also wonder whether suspects whose convictions would fall under the new statutes are more prone to use violence to avoid arrest.

Getting tough on drug offenders has also produced some unintended consequences. In certain jurisdictions, mandatory prison sentences even for low-level offenders, combined with prison overcrowding, have forced the early release of other convicts. Many observers have questioned the wisdom of freeing, for example, a violent

President Clinton signs a crime bill that, among other provisions, mandates a life sentence upon conviction for a third "serious violent felony" in federal court, September 13, 1994. Many states have also enacted "three-strikes" laws.

While a volunteer carries the baby she gave birth to behind bars, an ecstatic inmate wheels her belongings out of a maximum-security prison after serving a sentence for drug-related crimes. Mandatory sentences for drug offenders, which were enacted as part of America's "war on drugs," have contributed mightily to prison overcrowding and had disastrous social consequences, critics charge.

offender to make room for an addict or a small-time pusher with no history of violent behavior.

But, according to some researchers, stricter sentencing for drug offenders has had consequences that are far more detrimental than the occasional early release of violent felons. Drug sentencing policies have contributed significantly to the devastation of inner-city communities. In their Urban Institute report, William Sabol and James Lynch note that some urban areas saw an estimated 1.3 percent of African-American men aged 16 to 34 arrested and sentenced to prison for drug offenses in 1992 alone. And this, the authors maintain, has only accelerated community disintegration in a variety of ways. For one thing, an increased number of female-headed households and the absence of young men may increase juvenile crime by creating easier targets and removing informal social controls. Furthermore, after their release from prison, ex-convicts' employment opportunities are generally limited, which may encourage more crime.

According to Sabol and Lynch, there is no evidence that the more than tenfold increase in the number of prison sentences for drug crimes since 1980 has "produced measurable reductions in drug crimes." What it has done, they say, is fill the nation's prisons with people who aren't all that dangerous to society. Of the more than 150,000 inmates behind bars for drug offenses in 1992, for example, approximately 84 percent had no prior incarcerations for violent crime, and half of them had never before been in prison. In addition, one-third of drug violators in state prisons were sentenced for possession, not dealing. Moreover, the authors claim, the majority of street dealers, who are overwhelmingly young, have short criminal careers even when they aren't arrested and imprisoned. So not all the time they spend in prison is necessarily time they would be selling drugs.

Overall, it's difficult to quantify the effect of varying rates of incarceration on crime rates because so many factors apart from sentencing policies contribute to crime rates. Studies of California in the 1980s, during which the state added 100,000 convicts to its inmate population, reveal a decrease of 3.5 felony crimes for every extra year a convict was held in prison under tougher sentencing policies. The greatest proportion of this decrease was in burglary and larceny crimes; there was little reduction in the number of violent crimes. In an article that appeared in May 1996 in *The Quarterly Journal of Economics*, economist Steven D. Levitt of Harvard University estimated that for each additional offender incarcerated, slightly more than two violent crimes, in addition to a number of property offenses, are prevented. Public policy professors

Jacqueline Cohen and José Canela-Cacho, on the other hand, found that tripling the number of violent offenders in prison had caused just an estimated 9 percent additional decrease in violent crime.

And there is also the issue of recidivism, or repeat offending. Studies in different states have shown that between one-half and three-quarters of those released from state prisons were rearrested for new crimes within a few years. Is that an argument for even longer prison terms for greater incapacitation of criminals? Or does the prison experience itself cause additional and more serious criminal behavior? Some experts, such as the renowned psychiatrist Dorothy Lewis, believe it does. "[O]ur correctional system," she has said, "reproduces all of the ingredients known to promote violence. . . . In our prisons we have created a laboratory that predictably . . . reinforces aggression."

As a society, America faces some difficult choices. Between 1985 and 1995 the nation's adult inmate population grew at an average annual rate of about 8 percent. That rate of increase began to slow in 1995 and had dropped to 4.4 percent between midyear 1995 and midyear 1996. Between midyear 1996 and midyear 1997 the rate of increase rose a bit, to 5.9 percent, but remained well below the average annual rate of 7.7 percent for the 1990s. Whether this signaled the beginning of a long-term trend remains to be seen. Nevertheless, it should be emphasized that even as the rate of increase declined, a substantial number of prisoners were added to the total inmate population—nearly 95,000 between 1996 and 1997 alone.

Is more and more incarceration the best way for America to deal with its crime problem? Will we ever build enough prison cells? At what point, if any, do the economic costs of prisons become unacceptably high? At what point are the social costs too high? Opinions on these issues, not surprisingly, are deeply divided.

At one end of the spectrum are those who advocate

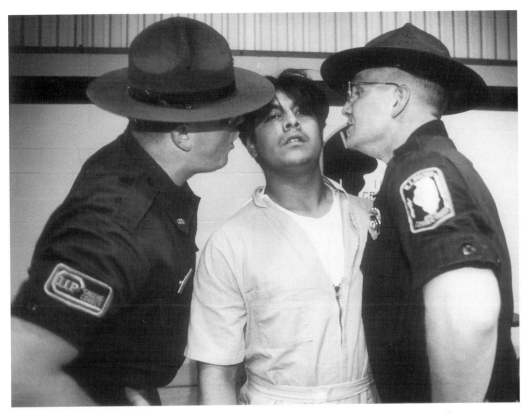

Functioning like army drill sergeants, two corrections officers get in the face of a young offender at an Illinois boot camp. Several states have experimented with boot camps as an alternative to traditional incarceration.

building as many additional cells as it takes to lock up all of the nation's dangerous felons. At the other end are those who insist that reducing the incarceration rate, particularly among minority groups, who make up a disproportionately high percentage of prisoners, must be a high-priority goal. Each group begins with different assumptions. Those who want more prisons and longer sentences have decided that rehabilitation doesn't work. They argue that, for the protection of society, criminals must be incapacitated through imprisonment. Many in this camp point out that even with the tougher sentencing laws enacted beginning in the 1980s, criminals—especially those convicted of violent crimes—typically serve only a fraction of their sentences (by some accountings, about one-half) before being paroled. And once out of prison, a large percentage of these men and women commit more crimes. A federal study that examined 156,000 state prison parole violators in 1991 estimated that they had committed a total of 124,000 crimes before being rearrested after an average of just 13 months of freedom. Among these crimes were 46,000 violent crimes, including more than 6,000 homicides. Although constructing and operating enough new prison cells to allow prisoners already incarcerated to be held longer while still keeping up with new prison admissions would cost taxpayers billions of dollars, the expenditure, proponents argue, would be worth it. It would prevent hundreds of thousands of victimizations, including many violent crimes. And, some economists have attempted to demonstrate, it would make sense purely from a cost-benefit perspective. Wildly divergent figures have been offered for how much money is actually *saved* through incarceration of criminals, given the

Two men under the custody of a Kentucky jail clean the floor of a local police station as part of a community-service alternative to incarceration. House arrest, work release, and community service are among the programs jails are using to relieve overcrowding and cut costs.

costs of their crimes; these figures range from about $20,000 to more than $400,000 per inmate for each year of incarceration.

Needless to say, not everyone accepts these assertions. Opponents say that, aside from the monetary costs of constructing, maintaining, and operating so many prisons and jails—and these costs are staggering—there is a tremendous social cost to expanded incarceration. That cost, they say, is measured in decaying urban communities, in the pain and suffering of families that have been broken up, in wasted lives. We've been sold on the idea that warehousing hundreds of thousands of lawbreakers is the solution to our crime problem, when in fact, critics say, we've only avoided dealing with the root causes of our high crime rate, which are economic and social in nature.

Many people who want to dramatically reduce the prison population favor using alternatives to incarceration in dealing with nonviolent and some first-time offenders. They argue that, in general, such offenders don't present an unacceptable risk to society and are often good candidates for treatment or rehabilitation. Their assumption, in contrast to the views of many pro-incarceration advocates, is that many offenders can be rehabilitated.

A number of jurisdictions have experimented with various alternatives to incarceration. By 1990 New York City and 20 states had instituted house-arrest programs, by which an offender serves his or her sentence at home and is allowed out only for specified activities such as work. Compliance is generally monitored by means of an electronic ankle bracelet. Another approach, work-release programs, allows convicts to live in the community on weekdays and report to jail on weekends to serve their sentences.

Community-service sentences require convicts to work a specified number of hours for the public good. The terms of these sentences often specify that the offender pay restitution to victims and reimburse the public for at least part of court or supervision costs.

Cognizant of the fact that many offenders on probation or parole are minimally supervised and thus have the opportunity to commit more crimes, a handful of states have launched intensive-supervision programs. Offenders in these community-based programs must work or go to school, live in a program center or meet frequently with case officers, do community service, pay restitution, and submit to random drug tests. Rules violations result in a jail or prison term.

Another incarceration alternative that has been experimented with is the boot camp. Instead of serving a longer jail or prison term, the offender—usually a young male—spends several months going through a military-style training program involving strenuous exercise and strict discipline. Officers function similarly to army drill instructors, continually confronting, berating, and intimidating the offenders. The idea is to break down offenders' personalities and replace their bad habits and attitudes with self-discipline and respect for the law.

By June 1996 nearly 80,000 offenders under the jurisdiction of local jail authorities—about 12 percent of the total jail population—were enrolled in alternative programs. However, even if the use of alternative sentences were expanded significantly, only a minority of convicts (those who had committed less-serious offenses) would be good candidates. And it must be emphasized that no alternative sentence yet tried is a magic bullet. In some alternative programs, the recidivism rate of offenders remains as high as that of similar offenders who receive traditional sentences; and even with the alternative programs that have documented success in lowering recidivism rates, a significant percentage of offenders will continue their criminal careers. What alternative sentences do offer are cost savings.

Some observers feel that the use of alternatives to incarceration makes the most sense with low-level drug offenders. Instead of incarcerating these offenders by the tens of thousands, opponents maintain, expanded use of treatment programs would be more humane—and also a better use of resources.

With nagging concerns about the cost of, and the conditions in, prisons and jails, it's not too surprising that the world's foremost capitalist society would eventually give private enterprise a shot in the corrections market. In the 19th century, when conditions weren't a concern but cost was, some prisons were privately run. And in this century many prison systems have contracted with private providers for medical care, counseling, and education of inmates. In recent years several states have built on these precedents, turning to for-profit businesses to build, administer, and staff prisons in the hope that a private company would be more efficient than a government bureaucracy.

In 1985 the Corrections Corporation of America (CCA) sought a 99-year lease to oversee the entire prison system of the state of Tennessee. For a flat fee of $250 million and a daily fee for each prisoner, this private company proposed to run the prison system in compliance with all prevailing federal court orders. Tennessee ultimately declined the proposal, but the idea of private prisons succeeded. In 1986 another company, U.S. Corrections Corporation, opened the first privately run state prison

The future course of American correctional policy will affect not just lawbreakers but all of society.

in modern times, a 300-bed minimum-security facility in Marion, Kentucky. The cost of $25 a day for each prisoner was already $6 cheaper than the state cost. By 1988 approximately 25 major state prison facilities and 5 federal detention centers of the Immigration and Naturalization Service were being privately operated. As of early 1996, according to Paula Mergenhagen, who wrote a piece titled "The Prison Population Bomb" for *American Demographics* magazine, 18 private companies were managing 90 state and federal prisons and 12 local jails, with CCA having the lion's share at 43 facilities. Most of the private corrections facilities were in the South.

How can private companies run prisons for less and still make a profit? Governments, both state and federal, have only an indirect interest in running prisons cheaply, because prison expenditures are just one item in a much larger, taxpayer-funded budget. And historically, public institutions expand rather than become more efficient when confronted with a problem. Private businesses, on the other hand, must be efficient to survive, and their efficiency is continuously put to the test by competition. Aside from these rather abstract generalizations, there are specific areas in which a private corrections corporation could save money. For example, labor is a major cost in any prison facility, and many corrections officers belong to unions, which negotiate higher wages and more costly benefits for their members. By paying its workers less, a private company can run a facility for less. In addition, because being a guard in a prison is an extremely stressful job, use of sick time is high, and administrators are forced to pay overtime to guards who cover coworkers' shifts. Simply by having a pool of backup guards who can fill in at regular-time wages for guards who call in sick, a private company can avoid virtually all overtime costs.

Although it may well be that private corrections companies *can* build and run prisons for less, the question remains: *Should* they? Many observers aren't sure. For one thing, because they are paid per prisoner, private companies have no incentive to help reduce incarceration rates. On the contrary, they have an interest in seeing more and more Americans behind bars. In addition, many people are concerned that private prison guards will be undertrained and unprofessional, and many legal experts feel that the government will still be liable for any prisoner lawsuits that result from their conduct. Then there is the question as to what extent private companies can impose their own rules on the prisons they run. Can they impose punishments on inmates to enforce these rules? Can a private company deny parole, or lengthen a prison sentence for misbehaving prisoners? If a private company injures or kills a prisoner, who is legally responsible, the state or the private prison corporation?

Aside from these practical considerations, some people also raise a philosophical objection to privately run prisons. We, the people—every member of society acting together—sentence our fellow citizens to prison terms for breaking the law. Incarcerating a criminal is a public act, and, some people feel, society's responsibility for that criminal cannot be handed off to a private organization at the prison gates. "In my opinion," writes political scientist John J. DiIulio Jr., "to remain legitimate and morally significant, the authority to govern behind bars, to deprive citizens of their liberty, to coerce (and even kill) them, must remain in the hands of government authorities."

Behind high walls and razor wire, prisoners live largely out of sight of the law-abiding, and in truth, most of us prefer it that way. But penal policy has profound social implications, and ultimately there is no escaping our responsibility for those we lock up. As the Russian novelist Fyodor Dostoyevsky wrote in *The House of the Dead*, "The degree of civilization in a society can be judged by entering its prisons."

Further Reading

Abbott, Jack Henry. *In the Belly of the Beast*. New York: Random House, 1981.

Dilulio, John J., Jr. *No Escape: The Future of American Corrections*. New York: Basic Books, 1991.

Earley, Peter. *The Hot House: Life Inside Leavenworth Prison*. New York: Bantam Books, 1992.

Fleisher, Mark S. *Warehousing Violence*. Newbury Park, England: Sage Publications, 1989.

Kauffman, Kelsey. *Prison Officers and Their World*. Cambridge, Mass.: Harvard University Press, 1988.

Keve, Paul W. *Prisons and the American Conscience*. Carbondale: Southern Illinois University Press, 1991.

McDonald, Douglas C., ed. *Private Prisons and the Public Interest*. New Brunswick, N.J.: Rutgers University Press, 1990.

Morris, Norval, and David J. Rothman. *The Oxford History of the Prison*. New York: Oxford University Press, 1995.

Rideau, Wilbert, and Ron Wikberg. *Life Sentences: Rage and Survival Behind Bars*. New York: Times Books, 1992.

Useem, Bert, and Peter Kimball. *States of Siege: U.S. Prison Riots, 1971–1986*. New York: Oxford University Press, 1989.

Watterson, Kathryn. *Women in Prison*. Boston: Northeastern University Press, 1996.

Zimring, Franklin E., and Gordon Hawkins. *Incapacitation: Penal Confinement and the Restraint of Crime*. New York: Oxford University Press, 1995.

Index

ANN G. GAINES, a freelance writer who lives in Gonzales, Texas, is the author of a half-dozen books for young adults. She has master's degrees in Library Science and American Civilization from the University of Texas at Austin.

AUSTIN SARAT is William Nelson Cromwell Professor of Jurisprudence and Political Science at Amherst College, where he also chairs the Department of Law, Jurisprudence and Social Thought. Professor Sarat is the author or editor of 23 books and numerous scholarly articles. Among his books are *Law's Violence, Sitting in Judgment: Sentencing the White Collar Criminal,* and *Justice and Injustice in Law and Legal Theory.* He has received many academic awards and held several prestigious fellowships. He is President of the Law & Society Association and Chair of the Working Group on Law, Culture and the Humanities. In addition, he is a nationally recognized teacher and educator whose teaching has been featured in the *New York Times,* on the *Today* show, and on National Public Radio's *Fresh Air.*

Picture Credits